Walking Together

Walking Together

Polity and Participation in Unitarian Universalist Churches

Conrad Wright

Skinner House Books
Unitarian Universalist Association

Printed in USA.

ISBN 1-55896-129-1

Designed by Suzanne Morgan.

Library of Congress Cataloging-in-Publication Data

Wright, Conrad
    Walking Together: polity and participation in Unitarian Universalist Churches / Conrad Wright.
    p.   cm.
    ISBN 10-55896-129-1
    1. Unitarian Universalist churches—Government. 2. Unitarian Universalist churches. I. Title.
BX9850.W75   1989
262' .09132—dc20   89-6359
                                                                        CIP

In memory of
Frederick May Eliot

Contents

Foreword   ix

1   A Doctrine of the Church for Liberals   1

2   Walking Together   25

3   Worshipping Together   37

4   Another Look at Corporate Worship   51

5   Autonomy and Fellowship   63

6   Unitarian Universalist Denominational Structure   73

7   Social Cohesion and the Uses of the Past   97

8   Unitarian Universalist History in the Church
       School Curriculum   111

9   The Mirror of History   121

10   The Role of the Clergy in the Shaping of Public Policy   131

11   Individualism in Historical Perspective   147

Foreword

Nearly all the addresses and sermons in this collection were prepared for Unitarian Universalist audiences. They almost qualify as "Sober Thoughts on the State of the Times Addressed to the Unitarian Community"—to borrow a title used by the younger Henry Ware in 1835. Although prepared for a variety of occasions, I like to think that they have some coherence, since they are concerned in various ways with the church as a social institution, and they attempt to address some of the issues posed for us by our practice of congregational polity. I have welcomed the stimulus presented by invitations to speak on various occasions. I appreciate the courtesy of those who earlier arranged for the publication of several of the items reprinted here. "A Doctrine of the Church for Liberals" appeared as a pamphlet published by the Unitarian Universalist Ministers Association. "Autonomy and Fellowship" was printed in the *Unitarian Christian*, Vol. 21, No. 2 (Summer 1966), pp. 6-12. "Social Cohesion and the Uses of the Past" and "The Mirror of History" both appeared in the *Journal of the Liberal Ministry*, the former in Vol. 5, No. 3 (Fall 1965), pp. 167-176, the latter in Vol. 8, No. 3 (Fall 1968), pp. 39-46. "Unitarian Universalist Denominational Structure" is a reprint of Paper No. 36 (1986), and "Individualism in Historical Perspective" is a reprint of Paper No. 9 (1979) of the *Unitarian Universalist Advance*. Special acknowledgment must be made to the *Unitarian Universalist Advance* and in particular to its president, Alice Blair Wesley, for encouraging the preparation of this collection.

1

A Doctrine of the Church
for Liberals

◆

Address at the annual retreat of the
Massachusetts Bay Unitarian Universalist ministers,
March 22, 1983

When I was invited to participate in this conference, I was told
that the general theme was to be the Doctrine of the Liberal
Church. I do not find that title on the final program, but I
accepted with that topic in mind, and I trust that it is still at least
part of your concern this afternoon.

I accepted, not because it is a new and unexamined topic of
discussion among us, for it certainly is not. There have been a
good many sermons preached with that title, attempting to focus
on the problem of description or definition. But such discussions
have often left me dissatisfied, as though somehow the right
handle to get a grip on the matter had not been found. So I
accepted, with the thought that I would be forced to try to figure
out why these analyses have so often seemed vaguely unsatisfactory.

The difficulty, I would suggest, derives from our eagerness
in such discussions to concentrate on the adjective "liberal," and
to take for granted and leave unexamined the noun "church,"
which it modifies. We try to construct a doctrine of the liberal
church by asking what it is that makes a liberal church different
from other churches. We characteristically answer in terms of
contrasts—theological, or philosophical, or sometimes quasip-
sychological—between liberalism on the one hand, and ortho-

doxy or evangelicalism or even mainline Protestantism on the other. The liberal church comes to be defined as one in which the adherents believe in values such as freedom, reason, tolerance, and individualism. The discussions easily move into high level philosophical abstractions about the nature of freedom, the limits of tolerance, the role of reason in religion, or the uses of diversity—abstractions that must have some attraction for us since we resort to them so persistently. But we end up restating the message of the liberal church, not constructing a doctrine of the liberal church; and the two are not the same thing.

Basic to a doctrine of the liberal church must be a general doctrine of the church. We must first ask what questions and issues must be addressed in developing a concept of the church generally, as a distinctive social institution. Only then are we prepared to ask whether there is a particular way in which those questions and issues are resolved that is appropriate for churches in the liberal tradition.

There is indeed a difference between a liberal church and other churches, and the message it proclaims is an important part of that difference. But so far as a doctrine of the church is concerned the difference is in the way it is organized and carries on its business, not in the theological differences between it and the Methodist church nearby or the Catholic church in some other part of town. If freedom, reason, and tolerance are important elements in our value system, and are at least part of the message we would proclaim, they must be important in shaping the way we do things together. Their meaning must be found in our ecclesiastical operations, not in the abstract philosophizing we do about them. Churches are institutions made up of men and women interacting in particular ways; and if there are values especially prized by liberals and distinctive of liberal religion, they must be expressed in behavior if they have any real meaning.

To adumbrate a doctrine of the liberal church means first to address questions that *any* doctrine of the church must deal with, and to then to ask whether there are distinctively liberal ways of answering them. We need first to be aware of what a doctrine of the church involves. We then can ask what happens when we apply the adjective "liberal" to it.

So what are the issues that appear over and over again in attempts to construct a doctrine of the church? Let me give some of the most obvious ones at the beginning, in outline form. Then the body of the paper will consist of commentary on them. I have no expectation of offering a rounded treatment of any of them, let alone a final answer. My purpose is rather to try to establish the framework of discussion so as to give it focus, by breaking the general topic down into a series of specific problems for which there are alternative solutions, some of them more appropriate than others for churches in the liberal tradition.

Here, then, are some questions to be addressed:

(1) What is the authority to be appealed to in matters of ecclesiastical organization? Scripture? Tradition? Reason? Practical experience?

(2) What constitutes a church? That is to say, what is the difference between a collection of religiously-concerned individuals and a church?

(3) How is the boundary of the church established? How is membership in it defined? What are the qualifications for membership? How are the qualifications of would-be members tested, and by whom?

(4) What leaders, or officers, are essential to the well-being of the church? And what is their relationship to the body of the members?

(5) Granting that ministers have an obvious responsibility to the churches they serve, what responsibility do they have toward their fellow ministers? Is the ministry a calling or a profession? Or both?

(6) Is some kind of community of churches essential to their well-being, if not to their being? How are particular churches related

to one another? What is the area of responsibility properly to be entrusted to denominational organization, and what kind of authority should be granted it?

These six question areas will structure the remarks that follow. But there are two other questions to be mentioned for the sake of completeness. Either one of them might consume our whole attention so that we would never get back to the first six; but it is not necessary to deal with them if the others are to be fruitfully addressed. They are:

(7) How are churches related to the larger society in general, and to civil government in particular?

(8) What are the central purposes of the church? Why do people bother to organize themselves into such bodies and struggle to keep them going? What functions does the church fulfill that could not just as well be fulfilled by other organizations?

Taken together, the answers to questions such as these will amount to a doctrine of the church. But there is one more preliminary comment to be made. We approach these questions in the context of a particular tradition, that of congregational polity, as accepted by the Massachusetts Bay Puritans three-and-a-half centuries ago, and as adapted to changing circumstances in the years since. No doctrine of the church is likely to be acceptable to us which does not acknowledge our continuity with that tradition. Sidney Mead has on occasion remarked that the only things Unitarian Universalists can agree on are congregational polity and Robert's Rules of Order. Congregational polity is acknowledged in the bylaws of the U.U.A. It is appealed to repeatedly in the time of conflict among us; it is a kind of shibboleth for us. But in the process, inadequate and sometimes genuinely distorted versions of that tradition have substituted for an understanding of its real meaning, its richness, and indeed its relevance. How often have we heard it said that congregational polity means "the autonomy of the local church," as though that were the sum and substance of it, and no more need be said?

In the remarks that follow, I shall introduce a historical perspective from time to time, partly as an aid to enrich our doctrine of the church but also as a reminder that congregational polity is older than liberal religion, and that it has involved various practice at different times and in different places, some of them ones that we would be unwilling to accept. Congregational polity is not, *per se*, liberalism. There are indeed ways of interpreting and practising this kind of polity that are appropriate for liberals, which is why we prize it and should prize it. But that is not automatically the case.

In short, it is not enough to suppose that congregational polity *is* our doctrine of the church, as though that took care of the matter. The assertion that we believe in congregational polity, even though true, has often blocked rather than opened the way to greater understanding.

(1) We begin with the question of the authority to be appealed to in matters of ecclesiastical organization. There is no ambiguity here as to the starting point. The Cambridge Platform (1648) states: "The partes of Church-Government are all of them exactly described in the word of God . . ."[1] It was because the Puritans could not find in the Book of Acts or the epistles of Paul any justification for diocesan bishops, or archbishops, or cardinals, or popes, that they rejected such hierarchical offices. Perry Miller has reminded us that this was one of the dividing lines between Puritan and Anglican. Anglicans like Archbishop Whitgift would acknowledge that doctrine must be scriptural, and that our knowledge of the way of salvation is revealed truth. But temporal arrangements such as the organization of churches are for human contrivance. In the matter of ecclesiastical polity, Miller has written, the Anglicans "found abundant and authoritative directions in the collective wisdom of Christianity, the

---

[1] "A Platform of Church Discipline" commonly referred to as the Cambridge Platform, was the normative statement of polity for the Massachusetts Bay Puritans. It is most conveniently available in Williston Walker, *The Creeds and Platforms of Congregationalism* (New York, 1893), p. 203.

interpretations of the Councils and the Fathers, the traditions of the Church. Moreover, they put forth speculations from more secular realms—arguments from reason, nature, from the law of nations, or from the character and origin of public society."[2]

In this respect, we have departed decisively from the position of our Puritan ancestors. This is not true of certain other denominations still adhering to congregational polity. The Campbellite churches in the early nineteenth century sought to restore New Testament Christianity, and the more conservative branch of that tradition still will not permit instrumental music in public worship or support denominational agencies, because there are no pipe organs or missionary societies in the Book of Acts. But we do not look to the Bible for a blueprint for the structure of local churches, let alone the U.U.A.

Many Unitarian Universalists would say that reason is our authority in such matters. I think that is in error. There are, of course, ways of structuring ecclesiastical institutions that we would reject as unreasonable. But within the range of rational alternatives, there is plenty of choice to be made on other grounds. What we actually do choose is the result of the interplay between tradition and practical experience. To be sure, the tradition began with Scripture, as understood in the early seventeenth century, and there are elements in our doctrine of the church to be traced back to that source. But the tradition has grown and changed over the course of generations in response to changing circumstances.

Admittedly, to ground polity on the authority of tradition, even when modified by practical experience, is to create problems of a certain kind. The tradition may lag behind the necessities of the times; the tradition is made up of various strands, not always harmonized; the appeal to tradition may conceal a hidden agenda. But to reject tradition and attempt to be rigorously rational is to uncover another range of problems, just as damaging if not more so. For the advantage of the appeal to tradition is that tradition can be made flexible, and that people who relate to the tradition in different ways may through it relate to one

---

[2] Perry Miller, *Orthodoxy in Massachusetts* (Cambridge, Mass., 1933), p. 43.

another. The appeal to reason as the sole source of authority easily becomes as dogmatic and divisive as the appeal to Scripture would be. A tradition that no longer meets our present requirements would be dead, and we need it not. But a living tradition, responding to present needs without denying its basic integrity, can serve us well.

(2) What constitutes a church? What is the difference between a collection of religiously-concerned individuals and a church? Here is the question addressed by the Cambridge Platform when it dealt with the "form" of the visible church. The chapter in question of the Platform follows the one dealing with the "matter" of the visible church—that is to say, the material of which it is made up. "This *Form*," says the Platform, "is the *Visible Covenant*, Agreement, or consent whereby they give up themselves unto the Lord, to the observing of the ordinances of Christ together in the same society, which is usually called the *Church-covenant* . . . "

So it was that when the New England Puritans gathered their churches, they wrote out covenants, by which the members agreed to walk together in mutual fellowship, in commitment to one another as well as to Christ Jesus, who was recognized as the supreme lord of his Church. They acknowledged that under some circumstances the covenant might be implicit, to be discerned not in a document but in the way people behave in relationship to one another. But "the more express & plain it is, the more fully it puts us in mind of our mutuall duty, & stirreth us up to it . . ."

The earliest New England covenants of which we have a record were simple statements. The Salem covenant of 1629 is as follows: "We Covenant with the Lord and one with an other; and doe bynd our selves in the presence of God, to walke together in all his waies, according as he is pleased to reveale himself unto us in his Blessed word of truth." While there are words here with theological significance, such as "Lord," and "God," and "his Blessed word of truth," it should be remarked that this was not a creedal statement. The operative words here are: "we . . . doe bynd our selves . . . to walke together." They are not: "we believe." So in a few of our churches, ancient covenants still serve their essential function: to make churches out of collections of individuals; to establish community.

The use of covenants, implicit or explicit, to define the nature of the church is characteristically congregational. Other kinds of polity may define the church in other ways. A national church, such as the Church of England in Puritan times, would declare that all the inhabitants of the territory, baptized in infancy, are *ipso facto* members of the church. This would not be an unreasonable approach to the problem in an essentially homogeneous society. But by accepting the congregational way, we have deliberately excluded certain alternatives that have commended themselves at various times to people no less rational than we.

When doctrinal divergence began to appear in the New England churches in the eighteenth century, after the Great Awakening, and there were Arminians as well as Calvinists in the land, creedal covenants began to come into use. The purpose was to maintain the purity of the churches, defined now in terms of adherence to particular theological formulations. This seemed to the liberals of the day to be an unfortunate development, if not a corruption of the congregational tradition. At any rate, we would no doubt agree that creedal covenants have no place in a doctrine of the liberal church.

The word "covenant" survives in some of our churches. Others have long used the term "Bond of Fellowship" as an equivalent, influenced by the formulation suggested by Charles G. Ames about a century ago. His wording of a Bond of Fellowship was as follows: "In the freedom of the Truth, and the spirit of Jesus Christ, we unite for the worship of God and the service of Man."[3] Some churches use neither a "covenant" nor a "bond of fellowship," but require subscription to the bylaws, which commonly have a statement of purpose at the beginning. It is functionally the same thing. One wonders how many new members under such circumstances actually read the bylaws and ponder the significance of the statement to which they have subscribed. In any case, there is a commitment to participate in

---

[3] *Charles Gordon Ames: A Spiritual Autobiography* (Boston and New York, 1913), p. 229.

the life of a community of religiously concerned men and women. And so long as the operative wording is "we unite," and not "we believe," the essential form of a liberal church is there.

There are two characteristic problems, however. One is that some Unitarian Universalists are so allergic to particular styles of language that if they see a covenant that is not in accord with their preference, they stop reading. Some "humanists" cannot get beyond the word "God," and some "feminists" cannot get beyond the word "Man," to see the words "we unite." I rather expect that the drive to degenderize our common language is such that sexist language in covenants and bonds of fellowship will largely disappear in due course. But I question whether it is desirable to spend as much time as we do in repeated rewriting of statements of purpose and preambles to try to accommodate changing linguistic preferences. There is a certain wisdom in *not* trying to find language on which all can agree; in a denomination as diverse as ours, that is a hopeless task, and in our churches we welcome diversity. Much better to have such statements couched in language that represents *nobody's* preference, that belongs to no faction, so long as the substance behind the language is correct. An ancient covenant, couched in picturesque antique language that everyone agrees is not written the way it would be if done afresh, has much to commend it. A common agreement to adhere to traditional symbols taken in a Pickwickian sense may be easier to come by than rational agreement.

The other problem with our covenants is that we do not take them seriously enough. We do not remind ourselves that a covenant is an agreement made between parties, not a statement by an individual to be discarded or forgotten unilaterally. A church united by a covenant is made up of people who have made commitments to one another. The Cambridge Platform reminds us of this in Chapter Thirteen: "Church-members may not *remove* or *depart* from the Church, & so one from another as they please, nor without just & weighty cause but ought to live & dwell together."

All of our churches have had the experience of admitting to membership someone who signs the book, is present off and on for a few months, and then silently disappears. The membership lists of our churches are filled with the names of persons who are not merely inactive, perhaps for good reason, but who have wholly dropped from sight. The Catholics may say: "Baptized a Catholic in the name of the Holy Trinity, always a Catholic." But that is in accord neither with our principles nor with the realities of the situation. We need to pay more attention to what the commitments are that are undertaken in a covenant relationship, and how they may be terminated. Joining a church should not be quite the same thing as joining the National Geographic Society.

(3) How is the boundary of the church established? How is membership in it defined? What are the qualifications for membership? How are they tested, and by whom?

Once again we start with the Cambridge Platform, which defines the "matter" of the visible church as "saints by calling." That is to say, given the distinction in the Reformed theology between the elect and the non-elect, it was the intention of the Massachusetts Bay Puritans to have their churches as nearly as possible made up of regenerate persons, excluding the unregenerate. The distinction between the elect, who are predestined to glorify God throughout all eternity, and the damned, who are predestined to suffer eternal torment, will of course not be clearly known until the Day of Judgment. But even though some hypocrites might creep in, and some of the elect through excess of scruple fail to seek admission, it was thought that a reasonable approximation of the distinction between saints and sinners is possible. On the basis of this calculus of probabilities the visible church was made to rest.

By what criteria was it to be decided whether an individual was regenerate? The Platform suggests three marks: a knowledge of the principles of the Gospel; repentance from sin and an attempt to lead a blameless life; and an experience of having been visited by the Holy Spirit, which turns the inner bias of the heart from worldly desires to a love of holiness. "A personall & publick *confession*, & declaring of Gods manner of working upon the soul, is both lawfull, expedient, & usefull . . ."

We no longer accept the Calvinistic doctrine of election and predestination, and so the original criteria have no relevance for us. Indeed, the liberal wing of the congregational churches in the eighteenth century already found it increasingly difficult to draw a clear line between saints and sinners. The movement away from regenerate membership began a long time ago. But as long as the former criteria prevailed, someone had to examine and try those who sought membership to see "whether they be fit & meet to be received into church-society or not." Who was it who was thought competent to pass judgment on the genuineness of a relation of religious experience? It was the church itself, acting through its chosen leaders. "The officers are charged with the keeping of the doors of the Church, & therfore are in a special manner to make tryall of the fitness of such who enter."

Setting aside for now the question of the role of the elders in the matter, it is important to note that each particular church had control over who was admitted to membership and entitled to share in the ordinances. In the Church of England, admission to full communion depended on confirmation by the bishop. Full access to church privileges required the participation of an external hierarchical authority.

In maintaining the right of each particular church to admit whomsoever it will to membership, we adhere to a very basic proposition of congregational polity. Twenty years ago, when Commission I of the Commissions of the Free Church in a Changing World attempted to define the rights reserved to the local church, the first one listed was "the right of the church to admit members in accordance with its own definition of qualifications."[4] The present bylaws of the U.U.A. would seem to be saying the same thing in acknowledging that the Association is not to infringe upon the internal self-government of member societies. This would seem to be an essential ingredient in what we typically refer to as the autonomy of the local church.

If it is recognized that it is the local church, not some hierarchical or denominational authority, that may define qualifications for membership, the question still remains: Who passes judgment on applicants? Who is to determine whether an individual is qualified and to be admitted, or disqualified and to

---

[4] *The Free Church in a Changing World* (Boston: U.U.A., 1963), p. 12.

be excluded? Some will respond that this is a remote question of no practical consequence, since we never do reject applicants. We are too much concerned to get people in to try to exclude anyone. A newcomer is likely to be invited by the minister to sign the church book the second Sunday he or she turns up for Sunday morning worship.

Two comments should be made here. First, a liberal church will not use creedal formulations to exclude persons whose theological views are not quite in line with the doctrinal position prevailing among its members. Nor will it introduce qualifications based on race, ethnic background, or national origin. There will be no mechanism by which the church itself, or some officers acting for it, passes judgment in such terms on applicants for membership. A church may well have a particular doctrinal coloring: one may be predominantly theistic, another humanistic; one may be explicitly Christian, another not. But it is for the individual to decide whether he or she belongs within that community, not for the community to decide whether the applicant conforms to its doctrinal preferences. No church can be all things to all people, and a policy of open membership does not require that it should. But the boundary lines are drawn by individual choices, not by official judgment. That would seem to be essential to a liberal version of congregational polity.

Second, if a church may not exclude any applicant on the grounds of wrong theological views, let alone wrong opinions on social or political issues, there are other grounds on which it may legitimately pass judgment on an applicant. But such other grounds are extraneous to the doctrine of the church and derived from quite different considerations. In constructing a doctrine of the church, we need to recognize at this point an intrusion into our way of doing things of an alien set of concerns, ones that may be hard to accommodate to a doctrine of the liberal church.

We have not thus far given a specific definition of the church, but we have described it as a covenanted body of religiously concerned men and women. There is nothing in that description, or the definition implied by it, that suggests that a church must own valuable property, whether real estate or endowments. A church may well be a small company of persons gathered for

worship and for mutual care and concern in the living room of
one of its members. To be a church, it is not necessary to have a
building, or to pay the salary of a minister, or run an annual
appeal. Some or all of these things may seem to us inevitable, but
that necessity does not derive from a doctrine of the church.

In actuality, our local religious communities function in two
spheres, operating out of two different value systems, which
may be in tension one with the other. One of these is the sphere
of the church, made up of a covenanted body of worshippers.
The other is the sphere of the corporation established by law,
with power to hold property for religious, educational, and
philanthropic purposes. The two are not the same thing, even
though the same persons may participate in both, and no formal
distinction is made between subscribing to the covenant of the
church and signing the bylaws of the legal body corporate. If our
doctrine of the liberal church forbids us to exclude anyone from
subscribing to the covenant of the church, our status as members
of a corporation makes us trustees for the administration of
property, with responsibilities that may be restricted to persons
competent to assume them. No individual can claim by right to
be admitted to a religious corporation and thereby become such
a trustee. A corporation may by law, and must by the exercise of
prudence, restrict voting membership to persons to whom significant responsibilities may be entrusted.

Once upon a time, the difference between these two spheres
was recognized institutionally in our churches. The "church" in
colonial New England was the religious body, while prudential
matters were entrusted at first to the towns, later to territorial
parishes, and finally either to poll parishes or religious societies.
Outside of New England, when Unitarianism spread beyond the
original territory, this dual arrangement was not ordinarily
transplanted. In New England itself, in the last century, the
difference between the membership of church and of parish
diminished, partly because of greater laxity in church membership and partly because of the transformation of territorial
parishes into poll parishes. Eventually, legislation was passed
making it possible for a church to be incorporated and have
parish property transferred to it, and this happened in some

instances. Elsewhere, the church as a distinct body atrophied, and the parish or society took over ecclesiastical functions in addition to its own prudential ones.

It is widely assumed that this was a desirable development. It eliminated conflicts between church and parish that had embittered the Unitarian controversy, such as the one in Dedham in 1819. It solved the problem of physical properties used for public worship being controlled by a remnant of the old parish who were now out of touch with the worship life of the church and perhaps unsympathetic with the forward-looking activities of a younger generation or an activist minister. But there was something to be said for a clearer distinction than we now make between the church as a religious community and the church as the trustee of valuable real estate. There are potential problems if an open-door policy with respect to church membership paves the way—as it has in some instances—to the misappropriation of property or its diversion to improper uses by persons who may join the organization but who do not respect, or indeed may not intend to respect, its integrity. One may conceive of a situation in which a church owning valuable property might be subverted by persons able to manipulate it to personal advantage. This is a problem that may seem remote if not irrelevant to a small fellowship owning no property and meeting in the local Y.W.C.A. But a lot of profit could be made for somebody, and not necessarily for the First Parish in Cambridge, if the meeting house on the corner of Church Street disappeared and an office building took its place.

(4) What leaders, or officers, are essential to the well-being of the church? And what is their relationship to the body of members?

Chapter Six of the Cambridge Platform makes it very clear that a church is still a church even if no one has been chosen to office: "there may be the essence & being of a church without any officers, seeing there is both the form and matter of a church." This can mean, specifically, that "a company of people combined together by covenant for the worship of God" is a church, even though there may not be an ordained minister to lead it. Every now and then one of our lay-led fellowships has adopted a legal title including the word "Church," and district executives have been known to cluck sadly over such presumption on the part of people who should know they are only a "fellowship." But the distinction between "Church" and "Fellowship" as it has appeared in the rules of the U.U.A. is a bureaucratic one, not an ecclesiological one. Indeed, quite apart from size, there are a good many fellowships that have come closer to the theological or ecclesiological understanding of a "church" than most of those designated as such.

But practical experience, as well as the Cambridge Platform, tells us that while officers are not necessary to the being of a church, they are most necessary for its well-being. Some of the several officers mentioned in the Platform have dropped from sight; the role of others has been greatly transformed. We no longer choose Ruling Elders or Ancient Widdows; while the Deacon, originally a fiscal officer, if he survives at all, now has only spiritual or sacramental functions, quite foreign to the original concept of the office. So our present concern may be limited to the ministry.

What is continuous from the time of the Platform to the present is the insistence that the church chooses its own leadership, and on this matter is not subject to outside authority. For the Puritan, it was important to insist that the right to designate who shall minister to a particular congregation belongs neither to diocesan bishops, nor to patrons of livings, as in the Church of England. For us it is useful to be reminded that when we insist that the choice of its own ministerial leadership is one of the things we mean by the autonomy of the congregational church, we must accept that the church may ultimately stand or fall by the wisdom of its own choice.

Properly, the church designates one of its own number to serve as its spiritual leader; and if it looks abroad for such a leader, he or she should join the church at the time of installation, if not before. The minister's primary relationship to the particular church is as an equal covenanted member. The special status as minister of the congregation rests on this primary relationship. (Not so in other traditions: in Presbyterianism, for example, the minister's membership is in the presbytery, not in the local church he or she serves.) If the minister gets into trouble and is dismissed, or retires, or resigns, he or she does not automatically cease to be a member; though needless to say a minister who has been dismissed is not likely to want to linger on as a member.

If we forget that the church chooses one of its own number to be its spiritual leader, we may slip into the habit of thinking of the minister as the employee of the parish. But it is the business corporations that hire employees and later fire them. Churches neither "hire" nor "fire" ministers. Ministers are "called," and if need be, "dismissed." They would do well themselves to avoid the terminology of "hire" and "fire," and encourage their congregations to do likewise. We sometimes hear ministers speaking of their "contracts" with their churches. That, too, is to adopt a vocabulary from a kind of organization with a different value system. It is important for ministers and congregations to have a common understanding of the nature of their relationship. But that understanding should rest on an ecclesiological definition of ministry, not on a negotiated contract, as though the minister were a member of a labor union.

For the authors of the Cambridge Platform, one could not be a minister without a congregation to minister to. "*Church officers*," we read, "are officers to one church, even that particular, over which the Holy Ghost hath made them overseers." The office of minister by definition involves a relationship with a congregation. There is no indelible imprint conferred by ordination, as in churches with a sacramental theology. But this "primitive" congregationalism, if I may term it such, no longer prevails. It surprises no one these days when young graduates of theological schools seek ordination immediately instead of waiting until they have been called to particular churches, as was once the invariable practice. It surprises no one when people are ordained who have no intention of serving a particular constituency, but propose a career of more-or-less religious journalism. or bureaucratic administration, or teaching.

What has been said thus far has implications for the doctrine of the liberal church, but what has been implied needs to be made explicit. By emphasizing that the minister is in the first place a member of the church like all other members, the basis is laid for a concept of democratic leadership. Admittedly, congregational polity is not necessarily to be equated with democracy. The Massachusetts Bay Puritans were not democrats, and their polity operated in such a way as to put a good deal of authoritarian control in the hands of the elders. If it was congregationalism, it was congregationalism laced with a strong admixture of Presbyterianism. The democratic element was the power of the election vested in the church members. But once in office, the elders exercised powers delegated by Christ and defined in Scripture, not powers latent in the people and entrusted on sufferance to the leaders. Democratic forms can be used in an autocratic way, as when some congregational ministers in the eighteenth century claimed veto power over actions taken in church meeting.

The minister in a liberal church is not there to hold the keys to the kingdom of heaven by admitting to the Lord's Table only those found worthy, as in churches that seriously accept a sacramental theology. Nor is he or she there to instruct the people in truths that the ordained clergy are peculiarly competent to expound, as in many confessional churches. He or she is there to live, and learn, and grow with the congregation. By virtue of special training and experience, the minister's word and example carry weight and earn the right to exercise leadership. That leadership may well make the difference between growth and decay for the church. But it is the possession of skill in democratic leadership, more than the adherence to a liberal ideology, that is the mark of the true minister of a liberal church.

(5) What responsibility do ministers have toward their fellow ministers? Is the ministry a calling to serve those to be ministered unto, or a profession with professional standards and obligations? And if both, can the demands of both be accommodated?

There are two ways of approaching these questions, one of them historical, the other institutional and structural. Let us take the historical way first.

In the seventeenth century, the congregational minister's identity was defined in terms of the relationship to the congregation. God may have called him to be a minister, but the church called him to minister to a particular congregation; so the ministry was a calling in a double sense. Ordinarily, when the minister took up his work in a given community, he remained there for life. He did not construct a career by serving a brief apprenticeship in one place, then move on to a church in a larger community with an ampler maintenance, and finally seek semi-retirement in some quiet country town. There are admittedly instances in the early years of ministers who served two churches successively, as when John Davenport of New Haven accepted a call in 1667 to the First Church in Boston. But that was unusual, and even then the move did not arise from career ambitions.

Students of New England church history have often remarked that a significant development in the late seventeenth and eighteenth centuries was the gradual professionalization of the ministry. Ministers who moved from one church to another, as began to happen with greater frequency, would find that the identification with their particular church diminished, and their self-identity derived from the concept of the ministry as a profession. The early ministers were hesitant about ministerial associations, as possibly leading to Presbyterianism. In the eighteenth century, such associations began to thrive and they increasingly exercised one of the basic prerogatives of a professional association: control over those seeking professional standing. True enough, the churches still chose their own ministers. But ministerial associations began to examine candidates and give them license to preach. A church seeking a young candidate would ordinarily look for one among the number of those approbated to preach by some ministerial association. Ordination came to be by the authority of ordaining councils, a procedure perhaps not inconsistent with the Cambridge Platform but certainly not envisaged by its authors. On such councils, though made up both of ministers and of lay delegates, the influence of the ministers was commanding. In Connecticut, this process went further than in Massachusetts, by the adoption in 1708 of Saybrook Platform, which received the endorsement of the General Court of Connecticut.

Someone has said that every profession is a conspiracy against the laity. Admittedly, the New England clergy never became wholly professionalized in those days. They never lost a sense of identity derived from the relationship with the local church—at least not until evangelical revivalism produced the itinerant revivalist, and expansion westward produced the wandering missionary. The historical process, therefore, left the minister with two competing obligations: to the congregation on one hand, and to the other ministers on the other. These competing obligations were not automatically in conflict, but the possibilities for tension were present. It may be argued that this was an ingredient in the Unitarian controversy, when moderate Calvinist ministers came under pressure from their evangelical colleagues not to exchange with liberal Christians. Thus Abiel Holmes of Cambridge, who had lived in harmony with his congregation for thirty years, succumbed to pressure from colleagues who were advocates of the exclusive system, like Jedidiah Morse and Lyman Breecher, and split the parish down the middle.

The other approach to this question of the ministry as a calling on the one hand, or a profession on the other, may be stated in terms of the procedures we follow in choosing and credentialling our ministers. We preserve the right of the local church to ordain whomsoever it may please to minister it. The bylaws of the UUA recognize "the exclusive right of each such society to call and ordain its own minister or ministers." Well and good: the church's act of ordaining is what makes a man or woman a minister. The ministry is still an activity to which one is called; it is still a "calling" in the familiar sense.

But if the individual in question has any notion of moving at some future time to another church, it will be necessary to be admitted to the profession as well as to answer a call. That means specifically being admitted to ministerial fellowship by the Fellowship Committee. When that status is granted, various professional advantages follow: assistance in making moves at various stages of one's career, insurance and pension rights, intangible but often very real support from fellow ministers in time of crisis. These professional advantages do not derive from the status of "minister," but from the quite distinct status of "in ministerial fellowship."

It is important to recognize that these are two different statuses, differently based. It is possible in our denomination to be a minister without ministerial fellowship, or vice versa. Many ministers, I suspect, do not make any clear distinction between the two statuses, but rather conflate them. In the process, the status of "in ministerial fellowship" tends to dominate. I, of course, watch from outside, since I am neither a minister nor in ministerial fellowship. So I tend to be a primitive congregationalist on this matter. So far as I am concerned, persons in ministerial fellowship who abandon the parish for a career, such as teaching—even teaching in a divinity school—are ex-ministers.

By distinguishing between ordination, which is reserved for the church, and the granting of professional status, which is done by the Fellowship Committee, we are able to protect the interest of the community of the churches without taking from the local church the basic right to select its own leadership. The community of churches needs to have some assurance that candidates will be qualified in terms of character and training. A church still may make its own choice, going outside the list of those in fellowship; but if it selects an unqualified person, it has only itself to blame if problems arise. And an unqualified minister is effectively limited to that congregation, with professional advancement closed off.

I am inclined to think that for liberal churches this is a more appropriate way of balancing local and denominational interests than the alternative adopted by congregational churches that are now part of the United Church of Christ. The power to ordain has there been transferred from the local church to the association. The association in this case is a territorial unit, comparable in scope to a presbytery, or a diocese, or a U.U.A. district. The action of a UCC association combines ordination and professional credentialing. For better or worse, the polity that results is a qualified Presbyterianism.

(6) Is some kind of community of churches essential to their well-being, if not to their being? If so, how are the particular churches to be related to one another? What is the area of responsibility properly to be entrusted to denominational or-

ganization, and what kind of authority should be granted to it?

There is more ambiguity than we like to admit in our response to the first of these questions. In theory, we acknowledge that our particular churches are part of a larger movement; in practice we are extraordinarily parochial. We organize the U.U.A. and form districts, but then give them inadequate support. We turn to denominational headquarters for assistance in connection with ministerial settlement, preparation of religious education materials, publication of hymn books, and for various other services; but it is the rare Unitarian Universalist who takes much interest in what happens to any UU church but his or her own.

We have allowed our understanding of congregational polity to develop in a narrowly parochial way. Then we tend to assume that that is the only way that it could develop: that our version of congregationalism *is* congregationalism. Sometimes, in reaction, denominational officials have been heard to rail against congregational polity, declaring that it has outlived its usefulness. I suspect that on such occasions what has happened is that a church has not conformed in some respect to bureaucratic rules and has disturbed bureaucratic routines.

It is the autonomy of the local church that so distresses the denominational official, and the protest against congregationalism arises from the assumption that the autonomy of the local church is what congregationalism is all about. It needs to be emphasized, therefore, that the autonomy of the particular church, by itself, is an inadequate definition of congregationalism. The authors of the Cambridge Platform knew better. They included in their text a chapter on "the communion of Churches one with another," which outlines six ways by which the churches were related in a seamless web with neither center nor circumference. The six are mutual care, consultation, admonition, participation, recommendation, and relief and succor. So congregationalism meant, as it should still mean, not the autonomy of the local church, but the community of autonomous churches.

We have come in this latter day to a truncated and impoverished understanding of congregationalism. We need to revitalize a sense of community. But it is not enough to do so simply by stressing the need for common support of the U.U.A. as a symbol of common allegiance, as well as an instrument for common action. It is not enough to suppose that our churches are adequately related to one another because each one independently sends a financial contribution to headquarters. That cash nexus is needed; but it hardly qualifies as a bond of union validated by our ecclesiology.

Originally, our churches were related to one another directly, by lateral relationships. Perhaps such relationships cannot now regain their former vitality and relevance, so fluid and anonymous has modern urban society become. Yet we would benefit if such lateral relationships could be strengthened. Two possibilities come to mind. The first involves the practice of pulpit exchanges. Our ministers do exchange from time to time, on a somewhat haphazard basis. But as a regular institutionalized practice, exchanges used to be much more important than now. In the early nineteenth century, it was quite usual for a minister to be away from his own pulpit about half the time. In the six months following his ordination at Charlestown in March, 1817, Thomas Prentiss preached fifty times, exactly half of them away from home. From October, 1822, through April, 1823, John Brazer of the North Church in Salem preached to his own congregation twenty-eight times out of fifty-three; eleven different ministers occupied his pulpit. To be sure, two services each Sunday were customary then, so the home church heard its own ministers just as often then as now. But each church also knew very well a dozen other ministers who regularly occupied the desk. What might be the result today if once each month each of our ministers exchanged with a neighbor, and then stayed to break bread with the chair of the Standing Committee? Continued year after year, so that the same guests were heard repeatedly, might we not rediscover some of our lost community?

There is a second device that might open up lateral lines of communication. Each church, following its annual meeting, should send to an appropriate lay officer or committee in every other church in the district a copy of the reports of the minister and chair of the Standing Committee. Or, if the church were unwilling to reveal its problems to outsiders with the same degree of frankness as in reports to its own members, a special report properly sanitized would at least acknowledge that we owe some sort of accountability to one another. I suspect that our district organization would indirectly be much vitalized as a result.

I have deliberately been focusing on the matter of lateral relationships because I think it is an aspect of our church life that has been much neglected. We have spent a good deal of time in the last quarter of a century reconstructing our continental association and defining the relationship between it and the churches. Two decades ago, in the midst of the reorganization following merger, Commission I worked at these issues at some length, and the distilled result appeared in compact form in the report of that commission, a section of *The Free Church in a Changing World* (1963). The analysis in that report still seems persuasive to me, and the UUA conforms in major respects to what was prescribed there. Specifically, four rights were there defined to be explicitly reserved to the local church, hence not subject to denominational interference: (1) the right of the church to admit members in accordance with its own definition of qualifications; (2) the right of the church to select its own leadership; (3) the right of the church to control its own property; and (4) the right of the church to enter freely and voluntarily into association with other churches. More might be said on these topics than is found in the published report of Commission I; indeed there is much of value in the working papers prepared by members of that commission which has never been published. But that report, as far as it goes, still seems sound to me.

So I venture to conclude with two paragraphs from one of those working papers of twenty-two years ago.

> There is a tendency among some to dismiss any consideration of ecclesiastical organization, and congregational polity in particular, as 'mere administration.' But sound administration of our common affairs is too important to be taken with anything but the highest seriousness. When we deal with church polity, we are dealing with people and how they ought to be related to each other. It

does make a difference whether we organize our churches—and our association of churches—autocratically, oligarchically, bureaucratically, or democratically. There is no point at which our most profoundly held insights and convictions as to the nature of Man may find clearer expression than in our religious communities and ecclesiastical organization.

Our hopes for the human experiment cannot be dissociated from our loyalty to principles of democratic self-government in church as well as in state. So far as church government is concerned, that loyalty requires of us an intelligent awareness of the richness of the tradition of congregational polity, a tradition that is far older among us than the liberalism in doctrine that we ordinarily cite as defining our characteristic stance among religious bodies in this country. We are fortunate because that in which we deeply believe, which we cherish both for its practical value today and its promise for the future, [when rightly understood] represents a fulfillment and not a repudiation of a rich tradition.

2

Walking Together

———————◆———————

Adapted from a sermon preached July 22, 1984,
First Parish in Cambridge

Walking together—what do these words mean in a denomination like ours, which includes considerable diversity of theological opinion, and which prizes tolerance of diversity?

The words come from the third chapter of Amos: "Can two walk together except they be agreed?" It is a verse of interest to us historically, for it was frequently cited by the orthodox opponents of our liberal ancestors at the time of the Unitarian controversy (1805-25). The response by the liberals has had a lasting importance, since it has helped to shape our tradition down to the present.

When the congregational churches in eastern Massachusetts split into two groups, eventually two denominations—the Unitarians and the Congregationalists—what was it that caused the division? The usual explanation is that a doctrinal or theological divergence got so great that the two factions finally broke apart. The doctrine of the Trinity was one of the points in dispute. The orthodox insisted on one God in three persons: the Father, the Son, and the Holy Spirit. The liberals replied that there is no basis in Scripture for the doctrine of the Trinity; that it is a corruption of Christianity, introduced long after Christ, and perpetuated by the creeds of the early Church. It is both irrational and unscriptural. God is one God; Christ is not one person of a triune God.

It can plausibly be argued, however, that the dispute over the Trinity was a superficial cause of controversy—that divergent views of human nature were more significant. The orthodox still adhered to Calvinistic doctrines of original sin and total depravity. The liberals replied that human beings are indeed born with a nature that makes them capable of sin—and many succumb to temptation—but they are born with a nature that is also capable of acts of righteousness, even of nobility. With the grace of God assisting them, they can struggle against sin and respond to the call for righteousness. To the orthodox view of the depravity of human nature, the liberals responded with a doctrine of the potential dignity of human nature. That is how the Unitarian controversy has often been represented: as a conflict between believers in orthodox, or Calvinistic doctrine, and those who held a more hopeful view of human nature. Their view, they argued, was more rational, more scriptural, and more humane.

But there was another ingredient in the debate, the one that the text from Amos speaks to. For the orthodox asked: Can two walk together except they be agreed? And since the Calvinists and the liberals were in sharp disagreement over the doctrines of the Trinity and of human nature, the answer of the orthodox party to Amos's question was: *No*—it is not possible to walk together with those who have diverged so radically from historic Christian doctrine.

The liberals responded by protesting this attempt to exclude them from Christian fellowship. To Amos's question, they answered: *Yes*—it is possible to walk in Christian fellowship despite theological differences. A Christian character is what makes a Christian, not the subscription to creeds that express doctrinal subtleties remote from practical living. William Ellery Channing gave an especially eloquent statement of the liberal position. "In vindication of this system of exclusion and denunciation," he wrote, "it is often urged, that the 'honor of religion,' the 'purity of the church,' and the 'cause of truth,' forbid those who hold the true Gospel, to maintain fellowship with those who support corrupt and injurious opinions." But Channing answered "that the 'honor of religion' can never suffer by admitting to Christian fellowship men of irreproachable lives, whilst it has suffered most severely from that narrow and uncharitable spirit which has excluded men for such imagined errors."[1]

Thus very early in our history as a separate religious body we insisted that creedal statements are not the proper basis for religious fellowship; more than that, that theological diversity is not only to be tolerated, but to be embraced as a good thing. This attitude, deeply rooted in our past, is part of our definition of what we stand for and hence who we are. We assert the right and duty of each one of us to adhere to his or her understanding of religious truth, and we accept the obligation to respect one another, even if we do not always agree. Some of us may be theists, some humanists; some may cherish Christian symbols and definitions of the human condition, others may find that the Christian tradition no longer speaks to them. We believe deeply in the capacity of men and women of good will to walk together in religious fellowship, despite such doctrinal differences. It is a deeply held conviction that it is possible to respect and even love our companions despite theological disagreements. Is this not what the statement of Principles and Purposes, approved in 1985 by the General Assembly, was trying to say in these words: "We covenant to affirm and promote . . . acceptance of one another"? In short, to Amos's question: Can two walk together except they be agreed? the liberals reply: Yes, they can walk together despite disagreements. And liberals often go a step further, to say that diversity of opinion is a good thing, which can be a source of creativity, even of life itself.

So the principle of the toleration of diversity has become axiomatic with us. But principle and practice are two different things. It is hard to live up to high principles without ever faltering; and we must admit that some of the most dramatic moments in our history have occurred when our tolerance of diversity wore very thin, and we were challenged to live up to the principles we proclaimed. In 1838, Ralph Waldo Emerson delivered an address at the Harvard Divinity School, which

---

[1] W.E. Channing, *Works* (Boston, 1841), vol. 5, p.376.

Professor Andrews Norton characterized as "the latest form of infidelity." It was "an insult to religion," Norton said in a letter to the *Boston Daily Advertiser*. Should anyone approving Emerson's doctrine seek to enter the Christian ministry, "he would deceive his hearers; he would be guilty of a practical falsehood for the most paltry of temptations; he would consent to live a lie, for the sake of being maintained by those whom he had cheated." Not many of the Unitarians of that day approved of Norton's rhetoric; but most of them would have agreed with him in drawing a line that excluded Emerson.

But there were younger ministers in the denomination who followed Emerson's lead rather than Norton's. One of them was Theodore Parker, who like Emerson soon felt the weight of opinion against him. A Transcendentalist, Parker rejected the prevailing view that Christianity is proved to be a divinely ordained religion because Christ's mission to reveal God's will to us is authenticated by the New Testament miracles. That was Andrews Norton's position. But Parker, like Emerson, declared that religion is not a matter of proof from the evidence of historical events, but is grounded on the inner religious consciousness. Christianity is true, not on the basis of the authority of Christ, but because, or to the extent that, it is an authentic expression of the universal religious impulse that all believers share. Views such as these, expressed in Parker's sermon on "The Transient and the Permanent in Christianity" and his *Discourse of Matters Pertaining to Religion* were regarded by most Unitarians of the day as undercutting the claim of Christianity to be a divinely revealed religion, and many if not most of Parker's colleagues stopped exchanging with him. A line was drawn. Ostracism Parker felt it to be.

The liberals believed in tolerance, yes; but tolerance only within the boundaries of Christianity. And on other occasions in the nineteenth century dispute arose over the attempt to define the limits of tolerance in precisely these terms. One of them was the Year Book controversy, which agitated the denomination in the 1870s. The Year Book, an annual publication of the American Unitarian Association, included a listing of ministers who were understood to be Unitarians. In 1873, Octavius Brooks Frothingham of New York noticed that his name was included, even though his church had declared itself to be an independent one, and he himself was committed to Free Religion—that is to say, to the radicalism of the free spirits who had organized the Free Religious Association in 1867 in protest against mainline Unitarianism. He asked to have his name removed. The Assistant Secretary of the A.U.A., a man named Fox, noting that other members of the Free Religious Association were also listed in the Year Book, wrote to half a dozen of them, asking whether they were included "with their knowledge and consent."

Among those to whom he wrote was the Reverend William J. Potter of New Bedford. He replied that his name *was* there with his knowledge and consent; that he did not agree with Frothingham that members of the F.R.A. should ask to have their names withdrawn. But he added that the list had been compiled by the officers of the A.U.A., using their own criteria for inclusion or exclusion; and it was for them to decide if his name was to be dropped. Fox was doubtless much relieved, and wrote back that he was glad to know that Potter could still be listed as "one who calls himself a Unitarian Christian."

Potter then felt compelled to make it plain that Fox had misunderstood his position, and that he did not call himself a Unitarian Christian. " 'Unitarian' of course I am with respect to the doctrine of the Trinity," he wrote back. "But 'Christian' I do not now call myself, and have so said in public." Whereupon the bewildered assistant secretary reached the conclusion that Potter's name should be omitted after all.

We cannot go into the details of the controversy that followed. The immediate upshot was that Fox's decision was upheld by the Executive Committee of the A.U.A., and approved by the members at their next annual meeting. The radicals of the denomination excoriated it for its bigotry; the conservatives took satisfaction in a reinforcement of its Christian identity. But eventually, ten years later, Potter's name was back in the Year Book—without arousing protest from anyone.[2]

---

[2] A brief account of the Year Book controversy may be found in Conrad Wright, ed., *A Stream of Light* (Boston: Skinner House Books, 1975), pp. 83-84.

What lesson is to be drawn from such failures to live up to our proclaimed principle of the toleration of diversity? The answer that immediately springs to mind, I suspect, is that we must renew our allegiance to principle and strive to do better. The ostracism of Parker and the injustice done to Potter are standing reminders of how easy it is to erect fences of exclusion, only to discover afterwards that the heresies of one generation have become the commonplaces of a later one. The underlying assumption is that the earlier disputes were a conflict between conformity (rejected as a bad thing) and diversity (embraced as a good thing)—a conflict between traditionalists who were not willing to entertain fresh ideas, and innovators who insisted that they were entitled to be heard despite their unconventional or radical opinions.

But there is another way of looking at that same historical record. From a sociological rather than a theological perspective, what was going on was the search for a basis for walking together on the part of a group of religious liberals who needed the support of one another if their message was to be heard and their influence felt. It was not really a dispute over whether or not boundary lines should be drawn. Rather, it was an ongoing debate as to *where* they should be drawn. William Ellery Channing complained that Calvinist theology should not be the basis for Christian fellowship; but he never rejected Christian fellowship, which was and is a limiting concept. Theodore Parker rejected the definition of Christian fellowship that most Unitarians of his day took for granted; but he condemned with vituperation and sarcasm the popular theology of election, predestination, and original sin. In every case, the real issue was not the abolition of boundaries, but the struggle of Unitarians to decide how to state what it was that united them; and that necessarily implied limits. It was the effort to determine what they had in common, and so to recognize how much and what kind of diversity they were able to tolerate.

If any community is to survive, and to accomplish anything, its members must have some common goals, some common purposes, a value system generally accepted, a consensus widely shared. What these controversies were doing was defining the boundaries of consensus. Boundaries may be fuzzy, but they are there. No group can include everybody; no religious group can satisfy the religious needs of all. By the recognition of boundaries we identify the part of the ecclesiastical landscape that we are prepared to occupy, and the constituency that we are equipped to serve. Boundaries change; they are not fixed for all time. The consensus that unites us today is not the consensus that united us in Channing's time. The disputes, which have sometimes produced an intolerance we later regretted, have been an inescapable part of the continuing process of redrawing the boundaries, of modifying a prevailing consensus.

So I submit that the orthodox had the right answer to Amos's question: Can two walk together except they be agreed? No, they cannot—unless they are agreed on at least a few things of overriding importance. It is when they can agree on some basic attitudes and values that they are freed to tolerate much diversity in other matters.

The record reminds us that there have always been very firm limits to our inclusiveness on theological matters. We have been tolerant of diversity within the going consensus, but quick to react when the consensus itself has been challenged. Even those who have sought to enlarge the consensus in some new direction have been merely changing the location of the boundary, not abolishing it. Andrews Norton thought the line should be drawn between those who believed in Christianity as a revealed religion and those who did not. Theodore Parker was content with adherence to a theistic position he called Absolute Religion which he adhered to with dogmatism comparable to Norton's, and with an equal lack of generosity towards those with whom he disagreed.

We sometimes hear it said that Unitarian Universalists are free to believe whatever commends itself to them as the truth; or, crudely, that they can believe anything they choose. But no church can encompass the whole range of theological options. Ours certainly does not, and we exclude some positions as dogmatically as if we had our own equivalent of the Westminster Confession. No one who genuinely believes in the infallibility of the Pope on matters of faith and morals is likely to feel at home in one of our churches. Nor would Jerry Falwell. The boundary is there, even if it is not guarded by creedal tests and excommunications. But with Robert Frost, we must always ask what we are walling in and walling out.

We have considered thus far a theological consensus, whose boundaries are defined through doctrinal disputes. But the consensus we share is not confined to doctrinal issues. It also involves values and attitudes we are more likely to express in secular than in religious language. In the period before the Civil War, the conflict between the first-generation rationalist Unitarians and the young Transcendentalists like Emerson and Parker was not the only source of tension within the denomination. Disputes over the slavery issue were also disruptive. Since there were few Unitarian churches in the South, there were very few outright apologists for the institution of slavery in the denomination. But there were sharp interchanges between the antislavery agitators calling for immediate abolition and the gradualists. The abolitionists, although never formally excluded by any act equivalent to excommunication, nevertheless felt under the pressure of opinion. They often found refuge in their antislavery societies, which served for them as substitutes for churches.

Similarly, some present-day Unitarian Universalists feel strongly about tendencies to insist on a definition of boundaries on social issues that excludes them as much as if they had embraced the doctrine of double predestination. An anonymous letter writer in the *UU World* in 1983 complained: "The Unitarian Universalist creed of tolerance ran smack in the face of reality. Visitors to the church who didn't follow the 'party line' were subtly excommunicated. An example was a pro-nuclear gentleman who stopped attending after being admonished for his views and socially ignored by church members. Openness to diversity on theological issues is not incompatible with intolerance on other matters."

Every denomination must have some way of understanding itself, some notion of what gives it its special identity. For Presbyterians it has been the Westminster Confession; for Episcopalians it was, at least until recent revisions, the Book of Common Prayer. For churches like ours, it is the covenant—not the words of any particular covenant, but the covenant relationship of mutual obligation. But unlike the Westminster Confession, which is an historic document, or the prayer book, which does not get revised very often, the congregational covenant must be renewed continuously. That means inevitably that there is a special intensity in the search for consensus. Congregational polity allows and encourages people of varied perspectives to come together; but it also requires them to find some essential basis for agreement if they are to stay together. There is no assurance that that will happen. Every time a new member joins a Unitarian Universalist church, the perspectives that must be accommodated are at least marginally affected. No wonder refugees from our congregations sometimes prefer churches of other traditions where the search for consensus is less demanding.

Between the extremes of stultifying conformity on the one hand, and of disintegrative diversity on the other we labor to find a place. Let us consider three suggestions as to how some kind of balance may be found.

The first is: to avoid making trivial matters a part of the binding consensus. This is not as simple as it may sound, since one person's trivia may be another's fundamentals. But one of the easiest ways of getting hung up in trivia is to insist on our own way as the only proper way to state a principle that all actually agree with. In our history we have argued repeatedly over vocabulary, as though the word were the thing, as though values we cherish could be stated only in our own chosen language. We need to discipline ourselves to penetrate beyond the language to see if there may not be genuine agreement at some deeper level. And we need to be self-critical, and ask ourselves whether what we are insisting on is really as important as, for the moment, we may think.

A second reminder is that part of our consensus is, paradoxically, what we have agreed to disagree about. That is, there are some questions, and not trivial ones only, that recur generation after generation, but which never find a resolution. An obvious one, which has been with us for 150 years, is the relationship of Unitarianism to the Christian tradition and to explicitly the Christian churches. Is there a minister in the denomination who has not preached a sermon entitled: "Are Unitarian Universalists Christians?" For that matter, has there been one in the last century and a half who has not preached some version of that sermon? If the time should come when that question is no longer at issue, the denomination will have changed in a very significant way; and I am sure that I would not be alone in regretting it.

But there is something to be heeded besides a simple willingness to agree to disagree on certain issues. An acceptance of diversity, an awareness of differences, is a constant challenge to us to widen our vision, to reexamine our unexamined prejudgments, perhaps even to learn from others. We need such challenges if our faith is to be alive and creative. But an atmosphere of trust is needed if the challenge of diversity is to lead to intellectual and spiritual growth, instead of to a hardening of old prejudices. A common acceptance of basic unitive values makes that possible.

The final reminder is that the consensus we share is created, sustained, and developed by persons who have chosen to walk together. We long ago rejected creedal tests for membership as a way to exclude those whose views are not quite in line with the doctrinal position prevailing among those already members. We have no mechanism by which an applicant for membership is examined or tested by some ecclesiastical authority to make sure that his or her opinions are acceptable. The boundary lines of our churches are drawn by individual choice, not by official judgment. There are risks involved, to be sure: King's Chapel ends up being somewhat different from a fellowship in California. Some people who join us find that they are in the wrong pew, and move on somewhere else—perhaps they go to the Quakers if we are too liturgical for their tastes, perhaps to the Episcopalians if we are not liturgical enough. But there are others who find at last a place where they belong. They are the ones whose individual perspectives may be added to enrich the consensus that helps to make a community out of a collection of unrelated individuals.

Can two walk together except they be agreed? Yes and no. How much diversity a church can tolerate without losing its sense of direction is a delicate question, not to be decided by abstract analysis. But consensus does not have to mean conformity; diversity need not mean surrender to the arrogance of those who insist that tolerance means that others must tolerate them, no matter how rigid and dogmatic they may be. There is much ground between these extremes. That is where we belong, seeking a straight way for ourselves, our children, and our children's children.

3

Worshipping Together

Sermon preached August 1, 1971,
First Parish in Cambridge

When we come together on Sunday morning for worship, we are participating in a pattern of ritual activity that has been carried on in this community for three centuries and a half. Since this church was gathered in 1636, it has assembled weekly for religious instruction and celebration. We take such continuity very much for granted, more so than perhaps we should. It is actually quite remarkable that there has been a worshipping community here whose continuity persists even as its membership has been constantly renewed. It is likewise worthy of remark that the forms of public worship used here, modified though they have been from time to time, have been revised within a context of continuity; so that there are elements in them that date back to the time of the founding of the church, and beyond.

There are those among us who find this situation not so much remarkable, as incredible. Inherited forms of public worship, they tell us, cannot help but be alien to modern perceptions and irrelevant in our present predicament. Such forms must inevitably soon disappear, to be replaced by new accents of the Spirit with which the modern mind feels more at home. The argument is often made that the survival of the Church as an institution depends, among other things, on its willingness to make radical changes in its patterns of worship. A church like this one, which is host to visitors from other parts of the country hears a good deal of such comment. Sometimes it comes from the visitor who feels a sudden urge to testify, when shaking hands with the minister following the service. Out it comes, à propos of nothing in particular: "Back home, we gave up using the Lord's Prayer long ago." (One might reply: "So did the Puritans who gathered this church, longer ago than that.") No matter; our visitor will sooner or later wander over to King's Chapel, whence he or she will emerge wholly speechless.

I suppose that people, when promised a sermon on corporate worship, will expect a discussion of this problem, the problem of how to update our forms and expressions of worship so as to reflect or express more satisfactorily the modern consciousness. There has been much ferment of this kind in many denominations. From the translation of the Latin mass into the vernacular to the introduction of folk songs, experimentation and innovation have been widespread. But the problem still seems to be how to find just the right spiritual wavelength to tune in on, so as to bring our decaying churches back to life.

This theme, at any rate, tends to recur in our discussions of worship. Here, for example, is a quotation from one of our ministers:

> . . . our worship services, ministers, congregations, and churches are in a state of decay. Slow death creeps over our church body and our movements are few and weak. . . . our orders of worship are stale, boring, and instead of giving the individual uplift and power to face life, they simply put him or her to sleep. We gather in meeting-houses which are uninspiring, which lack any artistic or contemporary expression. . . . we are content with dog-houses when we merely have to lift our eyes to see the treasures all about and for the price of courage and imagination easily available.[1]

There is something to this critique to which many of us

---

[1] Alan Seaburg, "Worship," *Unity*, 151 (1965), pp. 120-21.

readily respond. But we have here only the surface appearance of the problem, and to get at a solution we shall have to probe much more deeply. There is another, more basic problem of corporate worship that must be reckoned with. Why is it that forms of worship that we are told are dead and should be buried somehow seem to persist? Why is complaint so frequent when proposals are made to tinker with the order of worship? Why does King's Chapel cling to its anachronistic prayer book, which is so obviously antiquated? Does this indicate that its members are off in some little backwater, and not coming to grips with the forces shaping the world today? Or is the King's Chapel prayer book functional in a way its casual deriders fail to grasp, so that it is a matter of practical wisdom for members of King's Chapel to cherish it?

Another way of getting at the question involves historical analysis. Ours is not the first generation to declare that the Church is tottering to its fall, almost all life extinct. How successful were those who, in earlier days, made the same criticisms that we hear, and prescribed similar remedies? The classic statement of this complaint in our tradition is in Emerson's Divinity School address. "I think no man can go with his thoughts about him, into one of our churches," he declared, "without feeling that what hold the public worship had on men is gone, or going. . . . It is already beginning to indicate character and religion to withdraw from the religious meetings." The Transcendentalists who clustered around him sought various innovations in church organization and worship to bring life back into the dying body. Inspired by this impulse, a number of "free churches" were organized by men like Theodore Parker, Octavius Brooks Frothingham, Francis Ellingwood Abbot, and Thomas Wentworth Higginson. How many of them remain? Not one. King's Chapel has at least survived; and it is not beyond the realm of possibility that the prayer book may have had something to do with it.

There seems to be an element of durability in these antiquated forms that defies logic. It does, that is, as long as we probe no more deeply than we have. For we have subjected worship to theological analysis or to aesthetic analysis; and on either score our Sunday morning ritualistic activity can easily be represented as a collection of horrors. What we have not done is to subject it to sociological analysis, by asking what function it performs in the life of the social organism of which it is an expression. I propose to outline some of the implications of such a functional analysis, which may suggest why congregations persist in clinging to antiquated ritual forms. Under certain circumstances—though not under all—those forms may serve them better than up-to-date ones. A failure on the part of certain ministers to recognize that fact has, on occasion, contributed to the death of the churches they were serving. This approach involves an unconventional definition of the problem of public worship, which will lead to some unconventional answers to familiar questions.

What function, then, does the service of worship perform in the life of a congregation? The most likely response would be along lines such as these: It provides a vehicle for focusing the religious emotions of members of the congregation, for clarifying their religious ideas, and for reinforcing their religious commitments. It helps to sensitize them to what is of true worth in their lives. The result is that they may go forth strengthened and uplifted, better able to grapple with their personal problems, more sensitive to the needs of others, more capable of contributing to the establishment of a reign of righteousness in the world. This kind of response to the question takes seriously the notion that in a service of worship, worship is what is supposed to happen. But, alas, too often the hungry lambs look up and are not fed.

If we begin by assuming that the purpose of a service of worship is primarily to provide a vehicle for worship, then no wonder we are frequently disappointed. I should like to introduce the subversive notion that this is only one of its functions, and whatever we may think *ought* to be the case, it is usually not the most important function. There are some suggestive words along these lines in a pamphlet distributed by the U.U.A. "Many of us," remarks the author, "have confused worship services with worship. This is a most regrettable equation, for a worship service does not necessarily involve worship, and worship does not necessarily require a worship service." From which I draw the conclusion that a service of worship that may be an egregious failure in terms of worship may be a smashing success in other important respects. Hence the durability of the institution.

What then are some of these other functions performed by corporate worship? First, there is a public relations function, which helps to give the church a public identity among the religious groups in the community. Second, there is the function of reinforcing the social cohesion of the group itself, by providing common experiences and common symbols of discourse that help to make a community out of an assorted aggregation of individuals.

By emphasizing these functions of public worship, I am trying to remind us that one must have a community if there is to be a worshipping community. The fact of the community is primary and essential, since a worshipping community can survive as a community even if it ceases to worship. (Example: for years after the Farmington, Maine, Unitarian church ceased to operate, its Women's Alliance continued to meet regularly.) To understand the dynamics of a worshipping community, therefore, the place to begin is not with a discussion of the theology or aesthetics of its ritual forms, but with a sociological definition of what that church is or hopes to become. It is the sociological factors that define the limits within which realistic choice exists with respect to the theology or aesthetics of worship.

How does corporate worship help to give the church a public identity? Let us assume that you are a newcomer to a town, and know nothing of the churches. Let us assume further that you have resolved not to get trapped into one of them on the basis of a familiar denominational name only, but are going to do some sampling on successive Sunday mornings. The first Sunday, you encounter music sung by a quartet, an organ accompaniment, and a piano playing arpeggios. The next Sunday, there is a men's choir singing plainsong. The third Sunday you find a mixed choir and selections from a Bach cantata. The fourth Sunday, there is a folksinger and a guitar, with a highly personalized version of the evils of phosphate detergents. There are other possibilities; but this is enough to make the point. The chances are that three of the four will quickly be crossed off your list, and those churches will not see you again. If you are more broad-minded than most religious liberals, you may cross off only two of them the first time around. On the other hand, all of them may be eliminated, leaving you free for another familiar ritual, reading the Sunday *New York Times*.

Other aspects of the service of worship will correlate variously with the music. The use of fixed forms of prayer as contrasted with free forms; the choice of readings, whether or not they are biblical; even the vocabulary and diction of the minister—these also help to establish the public identity of the church. But let us concentrate for a while longer on the music. Our choice among the four churches, each with its distinctive musical style, is clearly not based on aesthetic discriminations, except insofar as such discriminations point to something much more important to us. Our choice is based on our awareness, whether we are honest enough to acknowledge it or not, that the church where we think we will find congenial people is likely to adopt standards in church music comparable to our own. And when we refer to people whom we will find congenial, let's not fool ourselves. We are talking about people drawn from our own social class, however that may be defined or identified.

We talk a lot about our churches being open to all, regardless of social origins. Religion, we say, should transcend human divisions of class, color, or national origin. We say that there is no reason why liberal religion should be thought of as a religion of the elite; it is a religion that can speak to the needs of the blue-collar worker just as much as the college professor. We sometimes even discover instances of particular Unitarian Universalist churches that are predominantly working class, and say: Look, our religion is for all sorts and conditions of men and women. But when we choose Bach instead of Moody and Sankey, that's not what we are saying. What we are actually saying is this: we welcome everybody, but most especially we welcome those who prefer Bach to "Amazing Grace" accompanied by arpeggios on the piano.

One response might be: let's be more inclusive, more democratic. If our morning worship is a symbol of class religion, we should try to broaden our horizons. How about Bach and "Amazing Grace" both? But then we run into the problem that it is the external community, rather than the church itself, that attaches a public identity to particular liturgical practices. The church may decide to abandon Bach for Moody and Sankey, but it is the external community that will have the last word as to what that signifies. So the church that decides to have both Bach and gospel hymns may think it is saying to the world that it wants more than one kind of person to join; but what it will probably be understood to say is that it wants those peculiar people to join who like Bach and gospel hymns both. This is not likely to be an effective strategy for rapid growth in membership.

All this is only the bare beginnings of an analysis of the ways in which public worship performs the function of establishing a public identity for a church; but perhaps it is enough to suggest the range of questions that emerge when we begin to look at worship, not theologically or aesthetically, but sociologically. Now we must turn to the second function of corporate worship, namely, to reinforce the cohesion of the social organism itself.

One way to get at this question is to remind ourselves that if a church is to survive, it must not only solve the problem of recruiting new members, but also the problem of holding on to them once they are lured inside. A public identity that will attract newcomers is all very fine; but what draws them in is not necessarily what keeps them there. Furthermore, the recruitment of new members involves recruitment from within, as well as from without. It involves a strategy for holding on to your children as well as for bringing in the stranger from without the gates; and the strategies may be far from identical.

What contributes to the sense of belonging of the deeply committed member? What is it that makes him or her willing to stay? Here, it seems to me, is where Unitarian Universalists are often sadly betrayed by their intellectualistic bias. They are most likely to assume that the social cement of the denomination is ideological. It is liberalism in theology, together with social concern. Doubtless there is some truth in this, but I am con-

vinced that we greatly exaggerate its importance. Social organ-
isms that coalesce on the basis of ideology alone are brittle and
transient. They do not survive unless they generate within
themselves sentiments, feelings, non-ideological—indeed, non-
rational—attachments. A church is not a thinking society, even
though it may, among other things, foster the intellectual life.

If it is not ideology that provides the cement for social
cohesion in a church, then what? Primarily, I would argue,
meaningful and supportive human relationships that are not
narrowly based on acceptance of an ideological consensus,
whether theological or political; relationships that make it possible for us to accept people with whom we disagree, to love
people despite their crotchets, and to forgive them their faults as
we seek forgiveness for our own.

Such human relationships arise out of shared experiences.
All sorts of things may go into such sharing; and the greater the
range of human concerns that it encompasses, the richer and
more lasting it will be. A September hurricane, even a widespread blackout, can temporarily make lots of strangers kin. A
more persistent social organism, like the church, must find ways
to extend the experiences its members share, both their range
and continuity over time. It will not be enough to define a
program for future action, a set of goals worked out by a
Committee on Goals, a common vision of the future, unless these
are also related to a sense of a common experience of the past. A
church which survives has to be a beloved community both of
memory and of hope.

Corporate worship is of course not the only mediator of
shared experience, but it is certainly one of them. I have a hunch
that it is because corporate worship helps to perform this function, which is so essential to the life of the social organism, that
corporate worship survives despite its critics.

How does worshipping together perform this function? In
the first place, there is the elementary fact of the shared experience of physical space. This particular church has been meeting
here for about 140 years; the interior of the meeting house has
been relatively unchanged for about 60 years. A lot of people
have experienced the height of the pulpit, the proportions of

pillars and balcony and ceiling, even the cushions on the pews. Two people who seldom speak to one another at the coffee hour after church have a relationship structured for them, which they did not have to create themselves, simply by the sharing of space. This fact will come out with great clarity when they meet accidentally somewhere else. They may scarcely deign to recognize one another here; but let them meet by chance 3,000 miles away, and you would think they were inseparable companions at home.

To be sure, some people do not attend Sunday morning services very often. Perhaps they are Easter churchgoers only; perhaps they show up only for an occasional wedding or funeral. The actual physical awareness of other worshippers is attenuated; there is not much left of worship as a shared experience, except the physical space identified with worship. Yet even when all else is stripped away, the experience of space itself remains a residual basis for a sense of identification.

But space filled with familiar faces concerns us more deeply. Those familiar faces are of course never all present at any one time. And some of the very familiar ones are present now only as shared memories. As I look down the center aisle, I see the pew where my mother sat for fifty years. Across the aisle, one pew back, is where Frederick Eliot sat after he returned from St. Paul to be President of the A.U.A. At my left, in one of the box pews, are Mr. and Mrs. Truman Hayes, members who could always be relied on to carry the burden of committee work and lay administration; I do not know what their theology was or what their political views were; that is not why they are remembered. On the side aisle opposite, just a couple of pews in front of Mr. Ingraham is Alfred Whitman, who never put any money in the plate when it was passed, because it was a matter of principle with him to give his full and generous contribution in his annual pledge. That was his amiable crotchet; and the ushers knew what to expect when they passed the plate. We love the things we love for what they are.

Each one of us has a unique perception of familiar faces, of course; but our various perceptions do overlap, and they are time-binding across the decades. No church lasts very long without them, no matter how up-to-date its theology may be.

But corporate worship has a cohesive effect not only because of a shared experience of physical space, and a common perception of familiar faces, but also because of common participation in ritual activity. And it would seem axiomatic that the more familiar the ritual, the greater degree of participation, and the greater the cohesive effect.

Participation in a service of worship is more than just knowing when to stand up and when to sit down, how to find your way around among the responsive readings, or being familiar enough with the hymnbook to join in singing old favorites. There is also the kind of participation that is an intellectual engagement with the minister as he or she reads the lesson or preaches. Thus opportunities for congregational participation are to be found in non-liturgical as well as liturgical traditions. There can be plenty of participation even in a silent Quaker meeting.

In any event, there is an obvious correlation between familiarity with the order of worship on the part of the worshippers, and the extent to which they can participate. The more accustomed they are to the order of worship, the easier it is for them to feel they belong. It follows that in a church that is a genuine community, there will be a treasury of accumulated liturgical fragments, readings, responses, and hymns, all of which are widely familiar throughout the group, and which are cherished regardless of whether they are the very latest thing, intellectually speaking, or the best thing, artistically considered. It takes time to accumulate such a treasure, and time for the newcomer to become aware of what it comprises, and so it is almost axiomatic that any religious fellowship that survives for as long as two decades will contain some archaic elements in its order of worship. That is why a minister may well choose a familiar biblical passage to read instead of an unfamiliar modern one—it can be a much more efficient medium of communication. Read an unfamiliar passage in an auditorium as big as this one, and the deaf man two-thirds of the way back will get one word out of three—that is, he will understand nothing. Read a familiar biblical passage, and if he gets one word out of three, he supplies the other two—that is, he understands and can participate. I would argue that there is something wrong with any church whose public worship does not lag at least a generation behind the current theological insights prevailing generally among its members.

The dynamics of the interplay between social cohesion and familiar liturgical forms is perhaps more easily seen in churches more liturgical than this one. Example number one: the Book of Common Prayer, which we encounter most often in the American variant used by our Episcopalian neighbors. If there is a world-wide Anglican communion—and I would agree with the Anglicans that there is—it is the prayer book more than anything else that has provided the common experience that has kept it together. The theological content of the prayer book has comparatively little to do with it. This very morning, thousands of Episcopalians are reciting the Apostle's Creed who don't believe more than twenty-five percent of the propositions in it. Example number two: the King's Chapel prayer book. Without it, King's Chapel would probably not have survived the disruption caused by the American Revolution; it surely would not have lasted into the present century.

Many religious liberals will probably respond that such a justification for the use of the Book of Common Prayer is simply an apology for intellectual dishonesty. It is shoddy business to make use of language and forms of worship that cannot be used with complete integrity. But I submit that when Episcopalians use the Book of Common Prayer in morning worship, it conveys more than one kind of meaning. There is its intellectual content, which falls somewhat short of crystal clarity, but is admittedly not couched in contemporary scientific vocabulary. But there is also its social meaning; and the message conveyed is that human solidarity means more than divisive issues in theology. There was a time, when Unitarians were less sectarian than they are today, when this was a major theme of their preaching. Admittedly, this meaning is not verbalized by the Episcopalians; but it is a quaint prejudice of academic people, especially, to think that meaning is only properly conveyed by verbal or mathematical symbols. The notion that in liturgical acts there may be social meaning and truth, as well as intellectual meaning and truth, is alien to us. I refuse to condemn as dishonest someone who seems to feel that in corporate worship especially the social meaning is the important thing. The very ascription of primacy to the intellectual content, at the expense both of aesthetics and of social meaning, betrays our class identity in a telling way.

One further point needs to be made in conclusion. We suggested that sociologically considered, corporate worship fulfills two functions. One is to contribute to the survival of the church by recruiting new members from the outside. The other is to contribute to it by reinforcing its inner cohesion, so that new members and birthright members alike do not drift away. The final point that needs to be made is this: that under present circumstances, these two functions often interfere with one another. These two objectives lead to different prescriptions for liturgical renovation. If we stress the recruiting of new members from outside, we need a form of public worship that will attract restless, dissatisfied people, unhappy with their present relationships or lack of them, hopeful that some other group will be more congenial than the Methodists or the Catholics or the Fundamentalists with which they were reared. It does no good to try to recruit a vestryman from Trinity Church. So the pool of available converts is one containing a high proportion of come-outers, looking for something that is new, at least to them, attracted by what seems to be openness, responsive to experimentation. Unitarian Universalist churches across the continent actually have recruited a good many such in recent decades. Breaking with familiar patterns of Protestant worship doubtless had a lot to do with it in particular cases and places. Hence the converts who have hang-ups over the use of the Lord's Prayer.

But the payoff questions are: how many of them stick, and how many of their children stick? These are questions that many of our churches that have experienced rapid growth have to confront, and at a time when ties of institutional loyalty have slackened. Now I am not one to say that institutional loyalty and institutional solidarity are ends in themselves, but they are a precondition to the achievement of other more important goals. And so a theory of corporate worship that is geared to the demands of social cohesion is something we very much need. Given our recent history, and the individualistic thread running through our tradition, it is clear to me that neither a merely traditional nor a purely innovative approach is going to work, but that various untidy compromises between the two are the best we can hope for, certainly better than stagnation on the one hand or suicidal discontinuity on the other.

The present mood in our churches is one of a Suspense of Faith, quite as foreboding as the Suspense of Faith of which Henry W. Bellows spoke in his famous address by that title a century ago. We were asked by denominational leaders not long ago to engage in a quest for Unitarian Universalist identity. In different language, this is what Bellows asked of his own generation. With him as the dominating figure, that generation found itself, and began to move forward again. Is it mere coincidence that Bellows was one of the few Unitarians in all our history who has had a consciously articulated doctrine of institutions, and an awareness of the role that corporate worship can play in strengthening the church as an institution for larger service?

4

Another Look at Corporate Worship

Sermon preached July 16, 1972,
First Parish in Cambridge

These are restless, uneasy, foreboding times in which to live. It used to be that social change came gradually, so that one could adjust to it, even if over the course of a single lifetime the world in which one lived was transformed. But now the pace of social change has quickened to such an extent that the attempt to adjust is often a threat to the individual's self-understanding. Some commentators tell us that we are so ill prepared to meet the future that it produces in us a condition akin to shock: "Future shock" is currently an "in" term. Other commentators wryly remark that now it is the children who must teach their parents, not the other way around.

In times like these, social institutions come under critical review, and understandably so; for it is quite possible for institutions that were viable for one age to outlive their usefulness. Those of us who bear some responsibility for the effectiveness of institutions of government, or education, or religion, are constantly being challenged and asked to rethink the undertakings in which we are engaged. None of these inherited institutions is immune, least of all the Church. The symptoms of churches in trouble are multiplying. We are told that attendance at public worship is dropping; we know that budgets are a problem, both locally and denominationally; the role of the minister has lost all clarity and the profession is in flux; and we are well aware that other denominations besides our own are likewise harassed and perplexed. Doubtless, the religious impulse in humanity cannot be eradicated; but that does not mean that the religious institutions that we have known will necessarily survive.

It was in the context of these considerations that I began, a year ago in this pulpit, an exploration of certain problems of public or corporate worship. For the argument is often heard that the survival of the Church as an institution depends largely on its willingness to make radical changes in familiar patterns of worship. Inherited forms, we are repeatedly told, cannot help but be alien to modern perceptions and irrelevant to our present situation. Innovation and experimentation must be the order of the day in worship if we are to keep up with changing times. To what extent is this true? Or under what circumstances is it true? These were questions we examined together a year ago.

Today's sermon is intended as a sequel to last summer's, likewise concerned with aspects of the relationship between the worshipping community and its forms of worship. I begin with a summary of the argument developed in last summer's sermon in order to emphasize that both are parts of a larger analysis, in which worship is viewed from a somewhat unconventional perspective.

Our starting point last summer was the question whether people have lost interest in the church because it clings to out-of-date modes of worship. The corollary would be that liturgical innovation is necessary to revive old loyalties and to attract new interest and support. Briefly outlined, the argument of the rest of that sermon ran something like this:

(1) Discussion of public worship and its problems has generally revolved around questions of theological content and artistic merit. The assumption is taken for granted, rather than critically examined, that if our services of worship can be brought up to date in these respects, the church as an institution will be in some measure revitalized.

(2) But can one actually demonstrate a positive correlation between liturgical innovation and institutional revitalization? The evidence is not unambiguous. Some churches have enjoyed

innovation and experimentation and thrived on it; others have apparently done better without it; some have even been destroyed by it. Instances can be adduced in which liturgical conservatism is the obvious explanation for the survival of churches; while other instances can be advanced in which the demise of a church was precipitated by injudicious liturgical experimentation. If we are going to prescribe the medicine for ailing churches, we had better figure out which cases will be benefitted by it.

Very pointed local experience bears on this matter. A lot of downtown Boston churches have disappeared in the last century. I think it can be plausibly argued that had it not been for the prayer book, King's Chapel would have disappeared 200 years ago, during the American Revolution; in fact, if had not been for the continued loyalty to the prayer book, King's Chapel would not have survived the movement of population from downtown Boston to the Back Bay and eventually to more distant suburbs in the decades after the Civil War.

It can also be argued that one of the things that hastened the end of the independent life of the Second Church was the attempt of a former minister to renovate its order of Sunday morning worship. This is not to assert that the Second Church had been a flourishing, healthy organism until that minister single-handedly destroyed it. Nor do I imply that the present relationship between the former First and Second Churches is not an appropriate and happy solution to a difficult problem. But, something was lost when the Second Church gave up its independent existence. It was the deliberate intent of a former minister to get rid of forms of worship that he regarded as not in tune with the modern spirit. What he prescribed would have been strong medicine for a healthy church; it certainly did not cure a sick one.

(3) It was suggested last summer that our difficulty in handling such problems arises from a failure to assess realistically the role that public worship plays in the functioning of the church as a social organism. When we concern ourselves with worship, we characteristically subject it to theological analysis, or to aesthetic analysis; and on either score our Sunday morning

ritualistic activity often falls short. Ordinarily, we do not subject it to sociological analysis. But when we do, we find that the Sunday morning service performs a number of functions in addition to worship that actually have very little to do with worship, but that are important to the survival of the group as a social organism. The inescapable conclusion seems to be that a service of worship that may be an obvious failure in terms of worship may be strikingly successful in other important respects. Theological contemporaneity and aesthetic sophistication may not be the most important criteria by which to judge the actual effectiveness of public worship.

(4) We drew the conclusion that when a church starts to re-examine its forms of worship, to see if alterations are called for, the place to begin is not with theological or aesthetic considerations, but rather with a sociological definition of what that church is or hopes to become. It is the sociological factors that set the limits of realistic choice with respect to the theology or aesthetics of worship. Each particular church is a social organism, which, if it is to be effective over the long haul, must have some concern for its own survival. Its public worship serves this matter of survival insofar as it operates to facilitate recruitment from without and to reinforce cohesion within. But no program of liturgical renovation will be effective unless these sociological parameters are kept in mind.

Now I will turn to another factor that limits the range of options of any particular church in matters of public worship. It is the factor of size. Specifically, I should like to suggest that there are important correlations between the size of a worshipping community and its forms of worship. The large church has a different range of options open to it—and on the whole a more restricted range—than the small church or fellowship. Of course, there are all sorts of gradations in between. But what will go great guns in a small and relatively homogeneous fellowship, still no more than ten years old, may well bomb in a larger church, which has been established in the community for generations. And if that does happen, it will not do to assume that the large church is run by old mossbacks, while the fellowship is made up of honest-to-goodness liberals. Size itself, quite apart from the character of the constituency, is a major determinant of modes of worship.

Much of what I have to say on this score will seem pretty elementary and self-evident. Yet sociological considerations, no matter how obvious, tend to be overlooked by religionists who discuss worship. If sociologists have been spending any time analyzing what actually happens in American churches on Sunday morning, I have not run across the results in the scholarly literature. For now, we must be content with a series of propositions and observations, well aware that they stand in need of criticism, as well as further articulation and refinement.

The first proposition is a very simple one: that a church, like any other group, can survive and be effective only if its members have some sense of common identity; an awareness of being like one another in some significant respect.

A common fallacy is to suppose that churches find their sense of identity chiefly in the adherence of their members to certain common religious purposes or principles. Actually, churches spend much of their time, not in drawing people together on the basis of already recognized and accepted goals, but in trying to promote a sense of common purpose among people who find themselves related to one another for all sorts of extraneous reasons. Usually common religious purposes are the end product of their participation—or perhaps even a by-product of it—having been brought together for all sorts of non-religious or even irreligious reasons. What are some of these non-religious bases for a fellowship that under favorable circumstances may come to be a religious fellowship? Some of them may be family tradition, ethnic solidarity, neighborhood proximity, social class identity. In a fluid, mobile, industrialized, and urbanized society like ours, social class is probably not the least of these, even though most church people shy away from facing that fact squarely.

So the first proposition is that a church must have some element or elements of common experience shared by its members, to unite them and make a community out of a collection of individuals. But while religious purposes *may* be generated in such a way as to reinforce a sense of common identity, more often than not the real cement that binds the group together is to be sought elsewhere.

The second proposition has to do with the relative size of groups. But first, we had better note parenthetically that the groups we are talking about fall into the category of voluntary associations. The proposition is that small voluntary associations tend to be much more homogeneous than large ones. They will be homogeneous in precise, and identifiable ways, and their homogeneity will be multiform. Large voluntary associations, by contrast, are less homogeneous; the basis for their cohesion can be less precisely defined and may even be obscure to the members themselves; and their boundaries are likely to be fuzzy.

It would not be hard, for example, to locate the basis for the identity of the Harvard Chess Club, and some of the components of its homogeneity. The basis for identity would be the activity of playing chess; while some of the elements of homogeneity would be age (roughly between seventeen and twenty-two); sex (mostly male); marital status (mostly single, whatever that may mean); occupational status (students at Harvard, maybe a few 'Cliffies); socio-economic standing (mostly middle class); race (mostly white); leisure-time preferences (not much interest in playing football); scholastic aptitude (verbal scores mostly over 698, mathematical scores mostly over 708); and so on. One is tempted to ask: Is it really because they are devoted to the game of chess that they feel so at home with each other?

Similarly, it would not be too hard to discern a good many respects in which the membership of a Unitarian fellowship somewhere in Wyoming is homogeneous, and to suggest a plausible explanation. There are good reasons why a rather small religious community of that kind should be relatively homogeneous, especially in its early years. For one thing, the process of initial formation and early recruitment is likely to depend a good deal on family and acquaintanceship networks. Like will recruit like, and Unitarians have never been noted for seeking out strangers in the highways and byways. Then, too, as long as the numbers remain small, the interpersonal contact within the group through which information is disseminated and attitudes are shared will operate widely throughout the whole membership. The processes of social interaction under such circumstances work toward increasing consensus.

But a larger church—which is more likely to be an older church—has a different problem of identity and social cohesion. Not only more people are involved, but more different sorts of people are involved. The larger church inevitably develops smaller subgroups, which at times seem only loosely related to one another. The processes of social interaction, which promote homogenization of attitudes and norms in the smaller group, cannot touch all members of the larger group equally or in the same way. So it turns out that there is not much overlap in membership, and there is some disparity in attitudes, as between the social relations activists and the Board of Investment. The common purposes of the entire body, of which these are subsets, get stated in remarkably vague terms, susceptible to widely varying interpretations.

It may seem that I have just given an explanation for the social cohesion of small groups, but left the existence and persistence of larger ones a mystery. Suffice it to say that the larger the group, the more it has to rely for its sense of continuity on such intangibles as the reinforcement of tradition, the memory of shared experience, the reassurance of familiar surroundings, and the repetition of familiar words, even if they have an archaic flavor.

So our first proposition dealt with the need for churches to develop a sense of identity and find a basis for social cohesion. Our second proposition dealt with the question of the size of churches, and some of the ways in which small religious groups differ from larger ones with respect to the basis for social cohesion. These propositions lead directly to the third proposition, which is concerned with the forms of worship of churches of varying sizes, and particularly with the effect of experimentation and novelty in public worship on their social cohesion and sense of identity.

The third proposition may be stated thus: Larger churches need to be on the whole conservative and formal in their patterns of worship; informality and hospitality to innovation, if they are to be found at all, must be sought in smaller groups. This, of course, does not mean that the conventional forms of the larger church must be highly ritualistic, or liturgically elaborate, since free church worship can also be very conventional. The issue here is not high church versus low church forms, but conventional versus innovative modes of worship. Note also that I am not saying that all small groups will be innovative; what I am suggesting, rather, is that if a group intends to structure innovation systematically into its worship, it must be content to remain rather small.

We are not talking here about the church, of whatever size, that indulges in occasional novelties on Sunday morning, setting aside the regular order of worship in favor of a special musical program or children's recognition day. That sort of thing presents no special problem to anyone. What we are concerned with is the insistent demand we so often hear for freshness, spontaneity, and creativity in worship, so that there is a feeling of failure unless each Sunday's worship is a new creation.

In the churches of our tradition, Emerson more than anyone else stands for this attitude towards worship. "The sun shines today also," he wrote. "Let us demand our own works and laws and worship." But Emerson understood man in solitude better than he did human relations; and he is no help to us when we try to understand the factors making for institutional health and vitality. Even Emerson's solitary individual would have been hard put to survive on spontaneous ecstasy alone, without some sound prejudices and well-ingrained habits to carry him along between the moments of insight. How much more true it is that groups of individuals can tolerate only a limited amount of discontinuity in their common life. If churches or fellowships try to build very much discontinuity into their common worship on a regular basis, rather than as an occasional departure, they will be successful only if there is a lot of stubborn continuity elsewhere in their common experience. Practically speaking, that means the kind of homogeneity found in small groups.

An example from local experience may be instructive. I shall not identify the church in question, because it is not a Unitarian

Universalist church. A nearby church, confronted with problems of adjustment to a changing social situation, decided that one part of a strategy for revitalization would be a more participatory and spontaneous mode of worship. Its leaders embarked on a lively program of experimental worship, and did so under rather favorable circumstances, with imaginative and energetic leadership and with access to resources in this academic community. In many ways, the results have been most encouraging. There is a new liveliness and creativity about the Sunday morning worship. People are involved in a way they were not previously; they do not simply wait as passive spectators for the experience of worship to be provided for them. Those of our own members who have visited there on a Sunday morning report a genuine sense of community.

But that is not the whole story, as the leadership of that other church is well aware. Good things are bought at a price. It is a very real question as to whether that church has been revitalized, or whether only a part of it has been revitalized. Newcomers have been attracted; but some faithful supporters of long standing have moved to the periphery or out altogether. The constituency that is active is much more active. But the total constituency is both smaller and different. The correlation between size and mode of worship has been achieved by shrinking the size of the constituency.

In many ways, this is all to the good. There is much to be said in favor of a small but vital group, compared with a larger apathetic one; and I do not doubt that the choices that were made by the leadership of that other church were not made blindly. But, that does not mean that the church has happily solved all its problems. The complicating factor is that the small, relatively homogeneous, lively group is a transitional phenomenon. A good many such phenomena die out and are forgotten. Others sooner or later opt for survival, whereupon they begin to lose that first fine careless rapture, the original homogeneity is diluted, the worship becomes routinized; in short, the organization confronts anew precisely the same range of problems the larger church had been grappling with right along.

Now to conclude with a few general comments. The overall tenor of the discussion this morning may have seemed traditionalistic, establishment-oriented, supplying justification for those who are disinclined to update antiquated modes and styles of public worship, skeptical of innovation, or at least skeptical of the optimistic claims and expectations of innovators.

One might respond, simply, that discussions of these matters among Unitarians and Universalists tend to be one-sided, and that it is proper to make a deliberate attempt to redress the balance. Most of us so automatically take it for granted that worship ought to be in tune with modern thought, and that a policy of innovation is the way to bring that about, that we are oblivious to the very real and socially useful functions that antiquated patterns of worship actually perform. It is sometimes a good thing to have one's unexamined presuppositions challenged.

But there is another response to be made to the complaint that we have devoted so much time to defending the status quo. Recall for a moment what the exact form of the argument was. It was that there are significant correlations between mode of worship and size of the worshipping community. Specifically, such aspects of worship as contemporaneity, novelty, experimentation, and so on, correlate with groups whose size is at the smaller end of the scale. *If* you have a small group with a clear sense of identity, you have the right environment for that particular emphasis. But *if* you have a larger worshipping community, the public worship of the group will express a different range of values.

We have said that the large church, if it is to survive, cannot be as innovative in its forms of worship as a smaller one, and that assertion sounds like defense of a conservative position. But we have not yet confronted the question that lies back of that one: Is the large church a good thing? Is it worth saving? It is when this question is confronted that one finds out whether the status quo is to be defended or not.

We have said that *if* we think it desirable to have fairly large churches, on the grounds that it is such institutions that will be strong enough to sustain themselves over extended periods of time, then we should not be surprised when they do not behave like newly-organized fellowships, but adopt more conventionalized patterns of worship as appropriate to their condition. We have said that *if* there are to be large churches, their public worship will fall into one segment of the whole range of possibilities; but *if* there are to be small ones, their worship will reveal predictably different emphases. But we have not yet discussed what the optimum size of a church is or what the various circumstances would be that would lead to varying answers to the question: How big should a church be?

As I see it, this is the real question that lies behind the discussions of worship, and it is one that needs to be brought out into the open if the problem of worship is to be handled realistically. My hunch is that the appeal of so-called innovative forms of worship these days lies not in the attempt at contemporaneity of theological content and literary style, or in an aesthetic judgment that folk songs or rock masses are better than Bach or Buxtehude. It is the small group, homogeneous, participatory mood of present-day experimental worship that accounts for its appeal. We need to ask ourselves why this is so—if indeed it is so—and what some of the consequences are likely to be for our churches, as they move into the closing decades of the century.

5

Autonomy and Fellowship

———————◆———————

Ordination Sermon for Louis Linwood Dees,
Dighton Unitarian Church,
November 7, 1965

In the life of one of our churches, a service of ordination and installation—as distinguished from a service of installation only—is a relatively rare event. In most of them, a full generation may well go by without there being any occasion for a service such as the one for which we have assembled this evening. And yet, to ordain a man or woman to the ministry is perhaps the single most important thing one of our churches may be called upon to do; and a service of ordination should be regarded as one of the most significant and solemn occasions that can bring us together.

The service is significant not merely because it happens so rarely, but because in this ceremony the distinctiveness of our pattern of church government is most clearly revealed. We think of a "congregational" church as a body of worshippers united by a covenant or bond of fellowship, which is autonomous and not subject to control by any ecclesiastical hierarchy. The critical point at which its autonomy is most clear is in its right to set apart, with appropriate ceremonies, one of its own number to minister to it as pastor and teacher. On such an important occasion, a congregational church will properly seek the advice and counsel of others; and to summon an ecclesiastical council is to adhere to a very ancient tradition. But the representatives of sister churches, whether gathered in an ecclesiastical council, or represented by denominational officials, may give friendly counsel only; they can neither give permission to ordain, nor can they withhold it. The responsibility for that decision—in this case, the responsibility for your decision—and for whatever may flow from it for good or ill, rests with the ordaining church.

And so it is that here the basic principles of our democratic form of church government find expression in a distinctive ceremonial act. This is therefore a proper occasion to review together certain principles of congregational polity that we so often simply take for granted. More specifically, I should like to discuss with you the relationship between the local church on the one hand, and the whole fellowship of churches on the other, as that fellowship is represented by the denominational authorities that we have established to serve our common needs. This relationship is deserving of examination because a number of episodes in recent years have revealed differences of opinion among us, regarding both the principles of congregationalism and their viability in the world in which we find ourselves. Is it not necessary—some have been saying—that the wayward particularism of individual churches be restrained, and a higher degree of responsibility to the common enterprise be established?

Recall, for example, the bitter debate in Chicago at the meetings of the General Assembly, in May of 1963, over the question of whether the Unitarian Universalist Association may require its member churches to maintain "a policy of admitting persons to membership without discrimination on account of race, color, or national origin." No one was heard to disagree with the proposition that every trace of racial segregation must be eliminated from our churches; but this particular proposal was sharply criticized as an assertion of the power of the Association to set doctrinal standards for its member churches, and to discipline or expel them for ideological irregularity. In reply, the supporters of the proposal declared that it would be intolerable to let congregational autonomy be erected into a shield for an indefensible and immoral social practice. Some observers felt that here was a conflict between two valid principles: congregational polity and social justice. Others insisted that it needed only a clarification of the principles of congregational polity to show that there was actually no conflict of values after all.

Another example of this debate is more recent. Some of you may recall that at our May meetings last spring [1965] in Boston, a resolution was passed which sought to put on record the prevailing consensus among us that our churches should admit to membership without discrimination people of all races and origins, and that diversity of opinion among us is welcomed rather than feared. The final wording of the resolution was as follows: "This Association and its members hereby declare and affirm their special responsibility to promote the full participation of person, without regard to race, color, sex, or national origin . . . and to invite full participation of all persons without any creedal test whatsoever." Two separate problems coalesced to produce this resolution. One of them was the continuing concern over the issue of racial segregation, which had stirred emotions at Chicago two years before. The other was a situation in a church in Providence, R. I., where, in the course of litigation counsel for one of the parties advanced the claim that belief in a supernatural being was a customary test for membership in a Universalist church. The resolution adopted by the General Assembly was intended to give an authoritative restatement of our commonly accepted position with respect to creedal tests, for the enlightenment and edification of the Court.

A few voices have been raised, however, questioning the propriety of this resolution, as another form of restriction on the right of a local church to define for itself its standards of membership. Is there not a conflict—some have asked—between these new resolutions and covenants adopted in some churches long ago, which still appear on their membership books? Are covenants creedal? Does this resolution mean that one of our churches may no longer use a form of words called a "covenant" or "bond of fellowship" as a basis for membership, if it is phrased in theological language, whether theistic or non-theistic?

A third illustration of current uneasiness comes closer to home. It has been the concern of the Department of the Ministry and of the Fellowship Committee of the Unitarian Universalist Association to raise the level of competence in the ranks of our ministers generally. Only those who are intellectually alert and emotionally stable can be expected to handle the pressures that bear in upon them in this peculiarly demanding profession. But how can these efforts succeed, we are asked, if the work of the theological schools is undercut by churches that ordain those whose formal training is not yet complete? Is not such exercise of congregational prerogative demoralizing to the esprit de corps of our ministers generally, and a potential danger to our movement at large? Can we afford to permit churches to exercise any longer this much congregational autonomy?

We may begin by noting that what we have called congregational autonomy is recognized explicitly in our basic constitutional documents. The Constitution of the Unitarian Universalist Association in one section specifically "declares and affirms the independence and autonomy" of local churches; and elsewhere it recognizes and affirms that member churches alone have the right to call and ordain their ministers. So the debate is not a question of the essential rights of the churches as acknowledged in the Constitution.

Nor is it really a question whether or not it is in the interest of autonomous churches to cooperate in support of our district organizations and the national headquarters. For, while we vest basic authority in the local church, we know full well that under present circumstances the church that tries to live wholly to itself is not likely to survive. There are many things which a single church may theoretically have the authority to do, and which it may find it must sometimes do for itself, which it ordinarily cannot do effectively except in cooperation with others. The training of the ministry is one of them: how many churches would be able to secure the ministerial leadership they need if they had to rely solely on their own resources? How many of our churches would be able to survive, simply in terms of membership, in a mobile society like ours, if those who move to other communities were not replaced in some measure by Unitarians and Universalists moving in, whose loyalties are already fixed and strong? How many churches have the resources to produce all the religious education materials they need, or to edit and publish their own hymnbooks? Whether the results of such common endeavor are satisfactory to everyone in all respects is not the issue here. One may properly ask whether the survival itself of the autonomous local church does not depend to a significant degree on its sense of responsibility to the larger fellowship of churches.

This emphasis on the larger whole, of which the local church is a part, is no new discovery. It was not invented by denominational officials trying to persuade the churches to increase their contributions to the budget of the U.U.A., even though this line of argument seems eminently sound and persuasive to them. Denominational organization, after all, is not much more than a century old, while the emphasis on the fellowship of the churches has been a part of the tradition of congregational polity from the beginning. In colonial times there were no denominational officials, no departments of the ministry, no denominational fund-raising appeals. Yet even then, the notion of an isolated church living to itself would have been regarded as an anomaly; the principle of autonomy was balanced by the principle of fellowship. In the Cambridge Platform of 1648 we find this unambiguous statement: "Although Churches be distinct, & therfore may not be confounded one with another: & equall, and therfore have not dominion one over another: yet all the churches ought to preserve *Church-communion* one with another . . ." Congregational polity, if true to its tradition, does not mean simply autonomous local churches; it mean the *fellowship* of autonomous local churches, which is a significantly different thing. The principle of fellowship and the principle of autonomy are both essential parts of the definition.

The Cambridge Platform goes on to outline six ways in which the communion of the churches may find expression. Two of them are relevant to the present discussion. The first of these is by way of "*Consultation* one with another, when wee have occasion to require the judgment & counsell of other churches." Such occasions might include the ordination of a minister, the request of a minister that he be allowed to relinquish his charge, or a controversy within the church that would yield only to mediation from without. The ecclesiastical machinery resorted to was the ecclesiastical council, in which the ministers and leading laymen of neighboring churches were invited to participate and give disinterested advice.

The other way of communion mentioned in the Cambridge Platform is termed *admonition*. This may be resorted to "in case any publick offence be found in a church, which they either discern not, or are slow in proceeding to use the means for the removing & healing of." In such cases, a neighboring church was entitled to remind the offending church of its fault, and if need be, to call a council of neighboring churches to deal with a matter that was regarded as one of common concern. Such a council could not interfere directly in the internal affairs of the offending church, but it could focus the power of opinion in a significant way. And more than this, if a question of doctrine or polity arose, agitating many of the churches, a synod representing all of them might assemble to seek a consensus. The Cambridge Platform itself was the product of such a synod.

For us there exists, as there did not exist for our ancestors, a regularly constituted agency for common action. We call it the Unitarian Universalist Association. Sometimes, perhaps when we are tired and exasperated, we think of it as a distant bureaucracy, and we berate it as though it were something alien that has somehow been saddled on us. Sometimes, in a more reasonable mood, we recognize that it is there to serve us, not merely with things like hymnbooks and religious education materials, but also with established and responsible agencies for the very same consultation among the churches that the Cambridge Platform insisted was a necessary aspect of the fellowship of the churches. But the U.U.A. is something more than an agency to serve us; in some respects it is actually ourselves, and it provides an organ through which we may state from time to time the consensus that prevails among us, so that the waywardness of particular churches may, if necessary, be rebuked, though not coerced, by the opinion of the whole. This is one of the things that the fellowship of the churches means: that the local church, while it is *free* to make its own decisions, is bound to make its decisions responsibly, with a decent respect for the considered judgment of the whole.

In conclusion, we may consider the application of these

remarks to the three concrete issues mentioned at the outset. The first issue was the one posed by the existence of a few segregated churches and debated at Chicago in 1963. The original proposal was radically defective in that, if taken seriously, it introduced procedures of accusation, formal trial, and coercion of the local church by the Association. Such procedures are normal in Presbyterianism; in Congregationalism they would have been a discordant intrusion. Despite a deep feeling on the part of many that the least taint of segregation was a cancer that had to be cut out regardless of other considerations, the proposal failed, and the General Assembly proceeded to set up a Commission on Race and Religion which has worked within the framework of consultation and admonition. The only remaining problem might be to explain better than was possible at Chicago why approaching the problem through consultation and admonition is more appropriate for us than the introduction of ecclesiastical courts and sanctions.

The second issue is that of the resolution passed in May, which comes up again later in the form of a constitutional amendment. It states the mind of the denomination on open membership policies. Some have raised the question of a conflict with the traditional use of covenants as the basis for admission to membership in some local churches. I would be inclined to argue that these critics are reading into the resolution something that the wording of it is actually intended to exclude. Nowhere is it stated that it is inadmissible for a church to have a covenant, or even a creed, if it chooses to do so. On this matter, the resolution could have been much more explicit in rejecting creeds, since the tradition of anticreedalism is actually a very strong one with us. What the resolution says is something that comes pretty close to being beyond dispute: We refuse to use creedal tests as devices to exclude from membership people who sincerely desire to associate themselves with us. We do not subject those who wish to join us to inquiry and inquisition to make sure that their theological views are in accordance with an accepted creedal formulation. The resolution does not even hint at any machinery of coercion or discipline of churches that use a covenant, or even of a hypothetical church, which might adopt something in the nature of a creed. It would be straining at a gnat to find in it anything but the legitimate use of the traditional method of stating the consensus of the group which may serve as an admonition to particular churches, but which does not coerce them.

Finally, there is the matter of the ordination by a church of a candidate to be its minister who has not met the requirements for fellowshipping with the denomination. At such a time, a church may properly be reminded that a minister needs not only a recognized status vis-à-vis the congregation, but also the sense of support that only full and equal acceptance by colleagues in the ministry can give. By ordaining, the church grants the former, but the latter comes only when fellowship is granted by the Association. The minister will be less effective in the life of the local congregation if he or she is not in fellowship with the Association. A church that proceeds to the ordination of someone who has not met the requirements for fellowshipping, should, out of pure self-interest, encourage him or her to meet those requirements and make that possible.

No one denies the right of the church to proceed to ordination if in its considered judgment the step seems wise. But it is the proper function of denominational officials to raise all the objections, so that the final decision will be a fully considered and responsible one. That is one of the things they are supposed to do, and no one should be surprised or offended if they do it. By the same token, it is the legitimate prerogative of the church to point out that while churches can make mistakes, so can denominational officials. And so if the gloomy warnings of denominational officials can help to curb irresponsibility on the part of churches, the right of the local church to ordain is a safety valve against the danger of bureaucratic myopia, and the occasional exercise of that right can be very healthy all around.

Congregational polity is ours by inheritance, but also by conviction. It commends itself to us as congruent with democratic principles we cherish. But with its values and virtues, we have to accept its characteristic problems and pitfalls. We might, of course, avoid some of the problems of extreme congregational particularism by adopting a more connectional form of church government. We could give the denomination some of the hierarchical authority that exists in other denominations. We could become Presbyterian, if not in name, at least in practical operation. But surely we realize that in this imperfect world there is no perfect form of church government. If we want the special strengths of Presbyterianism, we will have to reckon with *its* peculiar weaknesses. We struggle constantly with the typical problems and pitfalls of our form of church government. But take a look at the typical problems and pitfalls that go along with the advantages and strengths of other forms of polity. If you do, perhaps you will agree with the student of mine who considered changing denominations, only to decide that he would rather live with our particular problems and frustrations than with those of anyone else.

Let us then not regard this ceremony tonight as a trivial occasion, or one of merely local concern. In it both the fumblings and the faith of ten generations come once again into focus. In it the local church and the fellowship of churches are reminded of their mutual responsibilities. Let us make it the kind of occasion it should be, when we rediscover with clarity and new commitment some of the things that make us what we really are.

6

Unitarian Universalist Denominational Structure

———————◆———————

Address at the 1986 Fall Conference of
Unitarian Universalist Advance, Bethesda, Maryland,
September 27, 1986

The historical development of our denominational structures is a theme relatively neglected by our historians. In telling the story of the Unitarian controversy they emphasize the doctrinal disputes with the Calvinists over the Trinity, human depravity, and the way to salvation. The challenge by the young Transcendentalists of the next generation to the older rationalists is interpreted as a conflict over the source of authority in religion. In Universalist history the Restorationist dispute is featured. In accounts of both denominations the question of the relationship to the Christian theological tradition comes to be a central one. Throughout, the question of polity is largely taken for granted, as if congregationalism had been a constant throughout our history, so no more need be said.

Yet congregationalism as we have practised it has meant different things at different times. We too easily assume that our present version of it is what it has always meant. We need to take account of the fact that our polity has a history too. Since the way we order our common affairs is an expression of who we are and the values we hold, the history of our practice of congregational polity tells us much about ourselves, if from a different perspective than the history of theological controversies.

Let me anticipate briefly the thrust of the argument that

follows. We have inherited a very parochial understanding of congregational polity from colonial times, when the only purpose of extraparochial structures was the discipline of clergy and laity. In the nineteenth century, however, changed conditions made it necessary for all religious groups to assume additional functions, such as the education of persons for the ministry, the publication of tracts and hymnbooks, the preparation of religious education materials, the organization of new churches, and so on. These new functions called for organizations of a very different kind than any of the denominations had known. New institutional structures, bureaucratic or administrative rather than ecclesiastical, were developed to undertake new or enlarged functions.[1] While Henry W. Bellows and his contemporaries gave considerable thought to the significance of these developments, in more recent times little attempt has been made to articulate a doctrine of the Church for our denomination that provides a coherent rationale for what we actually do.

For Unitarians and Universalists, as for other denominations adhering to congregational polity, one result has been an especially acute tension between traditional local independency and a necessary consolidation of forces and centralized control. Furthermore, to the long standing resistance in congregational polity to hierarchy and centralization, there has been added the conflict between ecclesiastical structures and bureaucracy. The Church as a community of the faithful, and the denomination as a bureaucratic organization, are not the same thing, and there is an ineluctable conflict of values between them. Thus there are two sources of tension built into our present polity: parochialism versus denominationalism, and the Church versus bureaucracy. How this has come about is the concern of this essay.

The basic principle of congregationalism, which we have inherited from the Puritan settlers of New England, is that every particular church has full authority to order its own affairs.

---

[1] This subject is discussed with reference to Protestant denominations generally, rather than with particular reference to the Unitarians and Universalists, in Conrad Wright, "The Growth of Denominational Bureaucracies: A Neglected Aspect of American Church History," *Harvard Theological Review*, 77 (1984): 1-15.

Autonomy is the word we ordinarily use. The church itself admits members; once upon a time it disciplined them; it calls and ordains its own minister. Our Puritan ancestors would have said that each particular church is directly under the lordship of Jesus Christ as head of his Church, and that his authority is not mediated through hierarchical structures, whether of the episcopal or the Presbyterian sort. The Puritans were so wary of Presbyterian authority and control that they even looked with suspicion, at first, on ministerial gatherings or associations, lest they develop into presbyteries and usurp the independence rightfully belonging to the churches.

The Puritans did insist that independent or autonomous churches should walk together in sisterly relationship. In matters of ecclesiastical governance and discipline they properly ought to consult with one another. To define sound doctrine or discuss difficult issues in church government, a synod might assemble, as in the years 1646 to 1648 when a synod prepared the Cambridge Platform as a normative statement of congregational polity. To advise a church on matters of high importance it came to be the custom to call together an ecclesiastical council, made up of ministers and lay messengers from adjacent churches. By the eighteenth century, the practices and procedures of mutual councils had become fairly well standardized. While synods and councils were advisory only in congregational polity, and had no power to implement their recommendations or enforce their judgments, their purpose was discipline.

The function of extraparochial structures was similar in other traditions. Episcopacy, Presbyterianism, and congregationalism might differ in the extent to which they allowed for such structures and exercised control over local churches. But in each case the function was the exercise of ecclesiastical authority: the governance, the rule, the discipline of the Church.

What then is left out? Or left to other agencies in society? One thing, obviously, is the training of persons for religious leadership—that is, the education of the ministry. The Church is an institution that needs leaders with some degree of expertise. In colonial America the churches did not take responsibility for providing for their own trained leadership, but looked else-

where for it. The educational institutions that were founded—
Harvard, Yale, Princeton—had the training of religious leaders
as one of their purposes, and so have often been identified with
particular religious communities and traditions. But these
educational institutions, essential for the well-being, indeed for
the survival of the Church, were not structurally related to it,
directly sponsored by it, or financed by it. They were colleges,
preparing men for leadership in both Church and State. And
they had a corporate existence independent of the churches,
even when, as with the Presbyterians, there was a hierarchical
structure which later generations would use to mobilize resources in support of seminaries under direct control.

Education, then, is the first example of an activity that was
essential to the life of the churches but that they themselves did
not sponsor and control. A second example is the expansion of
the Church. What instruments existed in colonial America for
the support of missionary work?

There were some instruments, but they were organized
separately from the disciplinary structures. The missionary
activities of the Mayhews on Martha's Vineyard in the seventeenth century received support from the Society for the Propagation of the Gospel in New England. A later Society for the
Propagation of the Gospel, founded in 1701, was the instrument
for the expansion of the Church of England in the eighteenth
century. The S.P.G. was organized by bishops and may have
been run by them, but it was separate from the ecclesiastical
structure. The administration of affairs—the collection and
spending of money to advance the cause of the Church at large—
was not thought to be an appropriate exercise of ecclesiastical
hierarchies.

After 1800 there was an extraordinary expansion of the
"administration of affairs." But the instrumentalities resorted to
were, for the most part, not denominational or strictly ecclesiastical structures, but independent voluntary societies. Hence
there came to be two distinct kinds of extraparochial structures
existing side by side. One of them was the familiar denominational structure, more or less hierarchical, concerned with ecclesiastical rule and discipline. Among congregational churches,

this meant ministerial associations, ecclesiastical councils, and (in Connecticut) quasi-Presbyterian consociations of churches. The other kind of extraparochial organization comprised the voluntary associations organized for the administration of affairs. The most important of these, when organized on a national level by the evangelical churches, were sometimes referred to as the "benevolent empire," since the same men were often found serving as trustees or directors in more than one of them, so as to form a sort of loose interlocking directorate.[2]

The concerns addressed by the voluntary associations were various. Missionary expansion, both foreign and domestic, was regarded as of great urgency. The American Board of Commissioners for Foreign Missions was organized in 1810; the American Home Missionary Society in 1826. The publication of Bibles and tracts was a second field of activity. The American Tract Society was founded in New England in 1814, and reorganized on a national basis in 1825. The American Bible Society dates from 1816; the American Sunday-School Union began in 1824. Education for the ministry was supported by grants to promising candidates by the American Education Society (1826); while various aspects of the reform of society were addressed by such organizations as the American Colonization Society (1817), the American Peace Society (1830), and the American Anti-Slavery Society (1833). The range is from societies very specifically ecclesiastical in scope to others that may seem on the surface to be non-ecclesiastical, like the Anti-Slavery Society. Nevertheless, the social reform organizations may be understood as religious, by virtue of the sense of commitment of their leaders, their sacred texts, their rituals, their martyrs, and other cultic aspects of religious groups.[3]

The best known of the voluntary societies were organized by evangelicals, sometimes on an interdenominational basis. It is

---

[2] Standard treatments of the evangelical benevolent empire are: Charles I. Foster, *An Errand of Mercy: The Evangelical United Front, 1790-1837* (Chapel Hill, N.C., 1960) and Clifford S. Griffin, *Their Brothers' Keepers: Moral Stewardship in the United States, 1800-1860* (New Brunswick, N.J., 1960).

[3] See Douglas C. Stange, *Patterns of Antislavery Among American Unitarians, 1831-1860* (Rutherford, N.J., 1977), Chapter 2.

usually overlooked that the liberals adopted the same form of organization as the evangelicals for their own administration of affairs.   The American Unitarian Association was the liberal counterpart of the evangelical home missionary societies. It was a voluntary society of individuals with no structural connection to the churches, for the publication of tracts and support of missionary work, especially outside of New England.

How were the voluntary societies organized? All, including the A.U.A., conformed more or less to a standard pattern, one very different from denominational organization. The immediate model was plain: it was the British and Foreign Bible Society, which had been so successful as a device for the administration of affairs that its organization was replicated many times over. The specific arrangements were spelled out in great detail in a book by C.S. Dudley, an officer of the British Society, entitled *Analysis of the System of the Bible Society* (1821). This was a handy manual for organizers. It prescribed the duties of officers, and the requirements for membership. It provided sample texts of constitutions and bylaws. It explained how to organize auxiliaries of the main society in local churches. It told treasurers how to set up their accounts, and prescribed the form that financial reports should take. It was the staff manual of a fully developed bureaucracy, concerned with the rationalization of procedures so as to make possible the efficient use of financial resources.

Membership in one of these societies was open to individual subscribers; the societies were not related to churches or denominations either directly or by representation. Three dollars was a common amount for an annual subscription; thirty dollars for a life membership was the requirement in several of the societies. If one gave a larger amount—fifteen dollars annually or one-hundred and fifty for life—one might be granted the status of Director, with the privilege of attending meetings of the Board of Managers. The Board was elected by the society. In the case of the Bible Society there were thirty-six laymen, two-thirds of them required to be from New York, together with any directors who wished to attend, and ministerial members (later, ministerial life members only). The Board of Managers elected the officers: a president, who would be a distinguished layman to serve for public relations purposes; a dozen or more vice presidents from various parts of the country, also chosen for publicity purposes and to give the operation a national coloration; a secretary; and a treasurer. The secretary was invariably a clergyman, who ran the show together with a small group drawn from the Board of Managers. Out in the field auxiliary societies were formed, whose chief function was to collect money and turn it over to the national body. In return they were entitled to the services of the parent body, as when the Tract Society forwarded tracts to them for local sale, or auxiliaries of the Education Society nominated hopeful youths looking toward the ministry to receive its bounty. Enterprises of considerable scope were carried on in this way. The American Tract Society in 1850 employed 508 men as colporteurs under the supervision of superintendents. The Sunday-School Union in 1854-55 employed 324 men, 256 of them students.

The liberals followed this pattern in simplified form when the American Unitarian Association was founded in 1825.[4] The president was a distinguished figurehead: the aged but widely respected Aaron Bancroft of Worcester was chosen when William Ellery Channing declined. The bylaws allowed for fifteen vice presidents, though only nine were elected. They were geographically distributed from Maine to South Carolina, just as though Unitarianism had a nationwide constituency:

> Judge Joseph Story, Professor of Law and Fellow of Harvard College: also Associate Justice of the Supreme Court.

> Judge Joseph Lyman of Northampton, active in promoting liberal religion in the Connecticut valley.

> Hon. Stephen Longfellow of Portland, Maine; Member of Congress, 1823-25; father of Henry W. Longfellow and Samuel Longfellow.

---

[4] The fullest account of the organization of the A.U.A. is still George Willis Cooke, *Unitarianism in America* (Boston, 1902), pp. 124-138.

Charles H. Atherton of Amherst, New Hampshire, a prominent and successful lawyer in that state.

Henry Wheaton of New York; jurist, Supreme Court reporter; later a diplomat and expert on international law.

James Taylor of Philadelphia; merchant; a founder of the Philadelphia church in Priestley's time, who often served as lay minister there.

Henry Payson, Esq. of Baltimore, Maryland, a founder of the First Independent Church in Baltimore. A wealthy financier, he was a nine-term city councillor.

William Cranch of Alexandria, Virginia; Chief Justice of the District Court for the District of Columbia; Wheaton's predecessor as Supreme Court reporter. He was a first cousin and classmate of President John Quincy Adams, then in office; his daughter Abby married William Greenleaf Eliot and his son was Christopher P. Cranch.

Martin L. Hurlbut of Charleston, South Carolina, the leading layman of Samuel Gilman's church there, and his collaborator in the publication of a magazine called the *Unitarian Defendant*.

The work of the Association was carried on by the Secretary, with the cooperation of a small Executive Committee. The Secretary in the early years was Ezra Stiles Gannett, colleague of Channing at Federal Street, twenty-four years of age when chosen. The three members of the Executive Committee were James Walker of Charlestown, aged thirty-one; Henry Ware, Jr., of the Second Church, also thirty-one; and Samuel Barrett of the recently gathered Twelfth Congregational Church in the West End of Boston, thirty years old. The Treasurer was Lewis Tappan, aged thirty-seven, one of Channing's admirers, who afterwards returned to his inherited Calvinism, and moved to New York where he and his brother Arthur were leading figures in the evangelical united front.

The formation of the A.U.A. by a small but eager group of young men was a step towards the organization of the Unitarians as a community by themselves. It was only a step, however, and it is altogether too easy to think of it in terms of what it later became. It was a voluntary association of individuals, rather than an ecclesiastical structure deriving authority from a formal relationship with the churches. To be sure, Ezra Stiles Gannett spent a good deal of time organizing local auxiliaries, and at one time there were 150 of them. But the auxiliaries were made up of individual persons within the several churches, and were not part of the local church or parish organization.

The task of the Association was missionary work. Tracts were prepared for sale at low cost; a few missionaries, or "agents," explored the Midwest and remoter parts of New England to seek out liberals and support their efforts to form Unitarian churches. The Secretary of the Association carried on correspondence with ministers and local church leaders, and came to be a sort of clearing-house for supply preaching and ministerial settlement, even though such activities went beyond the original concept of the Association's mission.

But the Association did not presume to exercise ecclesiastical authority. It was not responsible for credentialling candidates for the ministry; that function was exercised, if at all, by ministerial associations. It did not authorize the ordination or installation of ministers; that continued to be done by the particular church on the recommendation of an *ad hoc* ecclesiastical council. It did not mediate or arbitrate disputes within churches or between a church and its minister; either the civil courts or an ecclesiastical council might be resorted to in such cases—though the failure of the Hollis Street Council in 1841 was enough to discourage that procedure. It was not in a position to make authoritative determination of doctrine for the denomination; when the Executive Committee, dominated by the very conservative Samuel K. Lothrop, sought to speak for the denomination in 1853 by condemning Transcendentalism, it had to acknowledge that its right to do so was questionable at best, and that right was promptly challenged.

Here, then, were institutions of two different kinds. On the one hand there were ecclesiastical institutions—churches, ministerial associations, councils—exercising ecclesiastical authority in a very decentralized manner. On the other hand, there was the A.U.A., on its way to becoming a bureaucracy, dependent for its effectiveness on a concentration of resources and centralization of authority over those employed to carry out its mission.

Side by side with these two contrasting kinds of organizations there appeared a third. It was the public convention, called to discuss the merits of a given reform and to influence opinion. Since each convention was separately organized, to deal *ad hoc* with a particular issue, it is easy to overlook the extent to which the conventions may be thought of as a distinct social institution, structured according to well-understood principles and following generally-accepted procedures. The sponsors would present for debate a series of resolutions carefully prepared by a business committee, dealing with a particular issue. As an educational device for the clarification of opinion, the convention bore some resemblance to a teach-in—except that the format allowed for genuine debate, while teach-ins are commonly used for the presentation of one point of view only. These conventions were certainly more responsible, intellectually and otherwise, than the hurried discussions of general resolutions we have come to know at business meetings of denominational general assemblies. The authority they commanded was an intellectual authority, based on the persuasiveness of the arguments developed, rather than on the faith that resolutions voted on by delegates assembled primarily for the transaction of denominational business are somehow a fair expression of the will of the churches.

It is generally forgotten that the Unitarians used the device of the public convention. From 1842 to 1863, they met annually in "Autumnal Conventions," each year in a different location, as far south as Philadelphia and as far north as Montreal. In the absence of a hierarchical structure like those of the Presbyterians or the Episcopalians, the Autumnal Conventions were the most significant *ecclesiastical* extraparochial structure of the Unitarians of more than local scope, as contrasted with the *administrative* or *bureaucratic* structure of the A.U.A. Admittedly, they were rather informal affairs, and could not claim the mandate from the churches that a representative body might have done, even though the participants were often referred to as "delegates" from the churches. Meeting in different parts of the country, they would attract a disproportionate number of people from nearby, as when sixty individuals from Providence attended the convention in New Bedford in 1848. But the format of the convention was well standardized.

Ordinarily the Autumnal Convention met in early October for two days. On Tuesday evening, there would be a service of worship, at which a well-known minister would preach. Wednesday morning, the convention would come to order and elect officers: a president, one or two vice presidents, a couple of secretaries, and a business committee. The Business Committee would shortly present for discussion a series of resolutions, perhaps as few as three. These would be debated with considerable formality, as in a parliamentary assembly, on Wednesday and Thursday. Wednesday evening would be given over to another sermon by a prominent minister. The convention would adjourn late on Thursday afternoon.

The propositions debated were usually phrased in rather general terms, but they opened the way for wide-ranging discussion of the denomination, its problems and its prospects. The first such convention, in Worcester in 1842, discussed three resolutions on the first day. The first acknowledged "with profound gratitude the success which has attended our labors in the cause of religious freedom, virtue, and piety" and enjoined all to persevere "with renewed zeal and energy." The second paid tribute to William Ellery Channing, who had died a fortnight earlier. The third resolved "That viewing with anxiety prevailing fanaticism and a growing disregard of public trusts and private relations, we should earnestly labor for a higher religious principle, and especially urge the paramount claims of moral duty," The next day, four resolutions were introduced, addressing practical problems of assisting young men preparing for the ministry; helping feeble parishes; distributing religious publications; and cooperating in missionary enterprises. At the end of the convention, Samuel May offered a resolution on the sinfulness of slavery, but the convention declined to address the issue because it had been introduced at a late hour when many were preparing to leave or had done so, and it had not been submitted to the Business Committee in regular order.[5]

The Autumnal Conventions get scarcely a mention in our denominational histories. Yet despite their informal character, and despite the fact that they drew participants only from New England and the Atlantic seaboard, they performed an important function. Doubtless the ministers did most of the talking, but the conventions were of laity as well as clergy, and promoted understanding among lay persons from many churches. The resolutions were often general in phrasing, but they provided a vehicle for discussion of very specific matters. One might complain that it was all talk and no action; but that might be said of many Unitarian meetings throughout the decades. At least the Autumnal Conventions allowed time for issues to be thoroughly discussed, without restrictions on debate of the kind that permit only the registration of conclusions previously reached and unaffected by the discussion.

The Autumnal Conventions never met farther west than Syracuse, New York. Beyond the mountains it was the Western Conference, founded in 1852 at a meeting in Cincinnati, that provided a comparable opportunity for liberals to assemble, to know one another, to explore their differences and formulate their agreements, to shape goals and reinforce loyalties. There was an important difference between the Autumnal Conventions and the Western Conference, however. The Conventions were open to all who chose to come and participate. The Western Conference was organized as a delegate body, in which the churches as such were represented. It was thus a continuing organization with a more formal structure than the Autumnal Conventions, and was related to the churches, as the A.U.A. was not. It foreshadowed future development in another respect as

---

[5] *Christian Register*, Vol. 12, No. 44 (October 29, 1842), p. 174.

well, in that it undertook to raise money for missionary purposes, and it aided struggling societies. In other words, the line between *ecclesiastical* functions and *administrative* operations was not clearly drawn, as it was in the East, where two distinct and parallel kinds of denominational structure were developing. In the Autumnal Conventions, there was a rudimentary kind of *ecclesiastical* structure; in the A.U.A., there were the beginnings of a *bureaucratic* structure. The Western Conference combined elements of each.

The Civil War was a time of heightened national consciousness in the North, and more than one religious body responded by strengthening its national organization. The Congregationalists formed their National Council in Boston in 1865; the Universalists reconstituted their General Convention that same year; the Methodists revised their government in the 1870s, when they adopted the report of their "Special Committee on the Relation of Benevolent Institutions of the Church to the General Conference." The Episcopalians found that the office of bishop could no longer be filled on a part-time basis by men whose chief responsibilities were to the parishes of which they were rectors, and bishops came to be full-time ecclesiastical functionaries with growing administrative duties.

Certain of the leading Unitarians were also concerned about creating a more effective denominational organization. Some of that concern derived from a sense of loss of direction and momentum in the 1850s, and a feeling that the denomination needed to do better if it was to take advantage of opportunities for making gains, especially outside of New England, that seemed to be opening up after the War. In the course of the Unitarian Controversy, from 1805 to 1825, about 125 of the churches of the Standing Order in Massachusetts went liberal. In the next fifteen to twenty years, that number doubled as a consequence of the work of the A.U.A. But then the growth tapered off. Unitarianism did not sweep the country like wildfire, as the ardent organizers of the A.U.A. had hoped it would. Churches were established in Baltimore, New York, Charleston, Louisville, Cincinnati, St. Louis. But missionary growth proved to be tougher work than originally thought. By the 1850s, the denomination was stagnant. In 1850, there were 251 churches. In 1865, there were 269.

What caused the slump? Samuel K. Lothrop firmly believed that it was the spread of Parkerism in the denomination.[6] Central to Theodore Parker's religious thought was the concept of Absolute Religion, which he declared to be dependent on "no Church and no Scripture," but on "the nature of man—in facts of consciousness within me, and facts of observation in the human world without." For Lothrop, this meant that Christianity could claim no special place among the religions of the world, and Jesus Christ was not the unique channel of divine revelation. But the real problem lay deeper. It was not the undermining of Christianity, as the conservatives of the day feared, even though that drove some, like Frederick Dan Huntington, out of the denomination. It was the spread of doubt as to whether institutional religion itself is worth while. That destroyed a lot of the inner vitality of the denomination.

There is a plausible case for the argument that Transcendentalism, which we have been brought up to applaud as a liberating force that emancipated Unitarianism from the old Christian apologetics of revealed religion attested by miracles, was not altogether a good thing. It brought an emancipation of the human spirit from old religious doctrines and formulations. But the price that was paid was a heavy one. It was the disintegration of institutional religion. It was the scuttling of the doctrine of the Church—that is, an understanding of the nature and necessity of the corporate religious life, of religious fellowship, of common worship. One cannot build a church on Emerson's dicta: "men are less together than they are alone," or "men descend to meet." Nor can one build a church on the basis of Parker's sermon on "The True Idea of a Christian Church." Parker does argue here that men (by which he means men and women) should hold great truths in common. But these are truths intuited individually by the Transcendental Reason, not convictions developed out of the mundane experience of living together. Parker talks

---

[6] Thornton K. Lothrop, ed., *Some Reminiscences of the Life of Samuel Kirkland Lothrop* (Cambridge, 1888) pp. 202-204.

much about individual freedom. But if individual freedom leads to a belief in the Trinity, or original sin, or Negro slavery, he will be the first to condemn, with sarcasm and vituperation, because he knows what truth is, and what freedom is supposed to yield. For both Emerson and Parker, then, a true community is not painfully constructed by people who have struggled to learn how to live together, but is made up of atomic and unrelated individuals who vibrate in harmony, not with each other, but in common with some realm of Absolute Truth out of time and space.

Of course, to all this tendency towards individualism and the fear of ecclesiasticism there were counterstatements. That meant that tension, both over doctrine and polity, was very much a part of the New York Convention in 1865, and continued to be a disturbing element in the life of the denomination until an accommodation was reached at Saratoga in 1894.

Most important of the Unitarian leaders who spoke out against the individualism of the radical wing of the denomination was Henry W. Bellows.[7] He was a churchman, an institutionalist, convinced that for religion to be effective, the work of the Church as an institution is essential. He had learned the lessons of effective organization as president of the United States Sanitary Commission during the War. In the absence of an effective Medical Department of the Union armies, the Sanitary Commission provided medical supplies, inspected hospitals, did social service work among the soldiers, assisted veterans to secure the pension rights to which they were entitled, and spent five million dollars raised largely by voluntary contributions and Sanitary Fairs organized by church people at home. This was, for Bellows, a thorough immersion in the problems of large-scale bureaucratic organization. From the experience of the war years he developed two convictions: that the opportunities for the expansion of liberal religion were opening on all sides; and that Unitarians would have to develop new instruments of

---

[7] Walter Donald Kring, *Henry Whitney Bellows* (Boston: Unitarian Universalist Association, 1979); Conrad Wright, *The Liberal Christians* (Boston: Unitarian Universalist Association, 1970), pp. 81-109.

common endeavor if they were not to be passed by and dwindle still further into insignificance. The A.U.A., as an organization of individuals, may have been well enough for the 1820s; it would not do for the 1860s and the decades to come.

What Bellows did was to engineer for the first time a denominational structure related directly to the churches, as the A.U.A. had never been, and by his energetic and imaginative leadership he enlisted others in its support. The New York Convention of 1865, of which Bellows was the leading spirit, founded the National Conference of Unitarian and Other Christian Churches. The National Conference did not replace the A.U.A., however; it supplemented it by providing a forum for common consultation and the determination of the policy for the denomination. It replaced the old Autumnal Conventions, which had to be reinvented each year, with an ongoing organization, made up of formally designated and credentialled delegates from the churches. As an ecclesiastical rather than an administrative body, it organized regional fellowship committees to review the qualifications of persons seeking recognition as ministers. But the A.U.A., the Sunday School Society, and similar organizations continued to be the bureaucratic instruments of the denomination.

The tendency in other denominations at this time was for the denomination in its ecclesiastical manifestation to take over the bureaucratic voluntary societies. With the Unitarians, it worked the other way: the bureaucratic organization eventually gained recognition as the central ecclesiastical body as well. This transformation in the nature of the A.U.A. took sixty years to accomplish. The first step was taken in 1884, when the bylaws of the A.U.A. were rewritten to provide for churches to send voting delegates to its meetings. Individual memberships were not discontinued, and indeed, churches were encouraged to pay dues to make their ministers life members of the Association. But the process was begun whereby the A.U.A. was to become responsible to the churches.

At least as important as this structural change, however, was the transformation of the internal operations of the A.U.A. achieved by Dr. Samuel A. Eliot, who became its chief executive officer in 1898.[8] He took the A.U.A. as a bureaucracy run by amateurs and professionalized it; he introduced controls and accountability into the management of its finances; he developed a sharply focussed program of expansion to replace the earlier method of perpetual doles to small churches that never seemed able to sustain themselves; he made religious education, publications, and social concerns into departments of the Association. The introduction of business methods into the affairs of the Association was the keynote of the early years of his long administration: "A corporation managed by ministers," he declared, "needs business methods more than work." Without denigrating Eliot's religious leadership, it must be acknowledged that his great strength was in administration. The skills he exercised might have been equally effective had he been the head of a great university, or a major philanthropic enterprise, or any other non-profit organization dependent on bureaucratic organization.

There was much in the Unitarian congregational tradition that was parochial and feared centralization; there was much in the Unitarian tradition of free religion that abhorred bureaucracy. Eliot encountered criticism on both scores. William Wallace Fenn opposed his election to administrative office in 1898 because he feared centralization. John Haynes Holmes led a movement to oppose his re-election in 1912 on the grounds that the A.U.A. had become a business organization and ceased to be a spiritual force. Even though the A.U.A. under Eliot always respected the principle of congregational autonomy, and never claimed hierarchical authority over the churches, the introduction of a principle of centralized bureaucracy into a denomination with a very parochial congregational tradition inevitably made for tension, which continues to this day.

The existence side by side of the A.U.A. and the National Conference—renamed in 1911 the General Conference—lasted sixty years. In that time the balance between the two gradually

---

[8] Arthur Cushman McGiffert, Jr., *Pilot of a Liberal Faith: Samuel Atkins Eliot, 1862-1950* (Boston: Unitarian Universalist Association, 1976), pp. 64-74; see also Eliot's successive annual reports as Secretary, then President, of the A.U.A.

shifted, as the vigorous administration of Dr. Samuel A. Eliot caused the A.U.A. increasingly to shape the denomination. A merger of the two organizations then seemed plausible, and it was recommended in 1923 to the General Conference by a special Committee on Polity. The change was effected in 1925, when individual voting memberships in the A.U.A. were abolished, so that it became at last what the General Conference had always been, a wholly delegate body responsible to the churches—or, to be precise, an almost wholly delegate body, since the voting rights of those of who were then life members could not be legally withdrawn.

The revised bylaws of the A.U.A. provided that in the fall of alternate years there should be a meeting of the Association away from Boston (where the annual meeting was regularly held in May) "to consider and act upon all matters for promoting the objects of the Association." These biennial meetings were conceived as a continuation of the old General Conference, and were an attempt to assure that its broader vision would not be lost in the administrative and bureaucratic concerns of the A.U.A. What the Conference had achieved by way of advancing that broader vision was underlined by the editor of the *Christian Register*. "It was and is the Conference," Dr. Dieffenbach wrote, "from which the principle creative thought and action of the free churches has emanated."

> It has ever been the guardian of our religious liberty, the foe of denominationalism, the doctrinal fount at which our leaders have drunk deep of the purest spiritual truth, the forum of unrestrained practical discussion and doctrinal disputation, and best of all, it may be, the quickening heart and will from which has largely come the missionary activity and the financial resources that have builded our name in heroic size throughout the country and indeed around the world.

Nine years later, when the Commission of Appraisal headed by Dr. Frederick May Eliot presented its report, it recognized the special value of the biennial General Conference meetings of the

Association. Their importance "should be enhanced in every possible way," it declared, "because they can devote themselves more readily than the annual meetings to the consideration of large matters of general denominational concern." The recommendations of the Appraisal Commission included the creation of a Standing Commission on Planning and Review, elected by and reporting to the General Conference meeting. The elected members of the Nominating Committee were likewise to be chosen by the General Conference meeting; and the Moderator, a new officer, would be nominated at the biennial fall meeting, even though for legal reasons the election had to be at the annual meeting in May.[9]

For reasons not altogether clear, the biennial General Conference meetings of the A.U.A. did not survive the process of consolidation with the Universalist Church of America. Their value had surely been indicated, since most of the thoughtful discussions of the pros and cons of merger, on the Unitarian side, had taken place at General Conference rather than at annual meetings. The crucial decisions at Syracuse in 1959 were made at a General Conference meeting. Perhaps, since the charter of incorporation of the new U.U.A. permitted business meetings to be held in any part of the country, which had not been the case with the A.U.A., one of the special advantages of the General Conference meetings no longer counted. Perhaps in the complication of merger discussions the special usefulness of these meetings got lost in the concern for other things. This was a very real blunder. In any event, the amalgamation of the bureaucratic and the ecclesiastical organizations into one structure was completed in 1961.

This historical survey reminds us that our present denominational organization, like that of other Protestant denominations, is an amalgam of two quite different sorts of structure; and it raises the embarrassing question whether the two are really compatible. One structure was developed for the governance and discipline of the Church as a community of the faithful. The

---

[9] Commission of Appraisal, *Unitarians Face a New Age* (Boston: 1936), p. 21.

other was organized for the administration of affairs. The Church I take to be a community under some kind of discipline, existing for the mutual strengthening of its own members, and for witnessing against unrighteousness in the world. The administration of affairs—such as the collection of money, the investment of endowments, expenditures for various services to the churches, pensions for ministers, publication of hymnbooks and journals, preparation of religious education curricula—calls for an organization on the model of the business corporation. The expansion of this function in the period after the Civil War moved increasingly in the direction of business corporations as models. Inevitably and properly so. Denominations are non-profit corporations, to be sure, and their ethos is not identical with that of I.B.M. But they still involve the development of bureaucracies, the rationalization of procedures, the concentration of authority, the hiring and firing of employees, and the development of the ecclesiastical bureaucrat rather than the spiritual leader.

Can these two functions be carried on by one structure without loss of clarity as to goals, and without internal tensions because conflicting value systems are struggling for mastery? It is a question that confronts us in a number of guises. It recurs, for example, in contests for the presidency of the U.U.A. Should we elect an invisible bureaucrat? Or should we expect the president to be a person of persuasive spiritual leadership? Not every generation has been able to produce a Henry W. Bellows or a Frederick May Eliot, with commanding stature in both respects.

A second example of the conflict of values when churches become bureaucracies is found in the perennial question whether the denominational body should take a stand on issues of public concern going beyond matters in which its own operations are involved. Most church people would agree that it is quite proper for a church or a denomination in its ecclesiastical capacity to be concerned with the application of religious insights to social issues and problems, and to condemn evil wherever it may be found. But the responsibility of a bureaucracy is more limited: it is to put its own house in order, not to reform the world at large.

When a General Assembly or similar body passes a resolution condemning apartheid in South Africa as a violation of human rights, it is acting as a Church may properly act in order to witness against moral evil. But as a bureaucracy, on the other hand, the most it must do is to consider divestment with respect to its own endowment fund. That is the part of the problem that is within its own jurisdiction, for which it may be held accountable.

There are always delegates to General Assemblies who will mutter that the denomination in its plenary sessions has no business passing general resolutions aimed at telling other people how immoral they are, and prescribing for them what they must do to become righteous. It is customary to condemn such delegates as reactionaries who by their reluctance to speak out are sanctioning moral evil. Sometimes the complaint is that such reactionaries have a much too narrow understanding of religion, defining it simply in terms of individual piety and morality. These accusations may well be valid in particular cases. But there is an element in the situation that is often overlooked. Those who want to make the public pronouncement are assuming that the denominational structure is an ecclesiastical one, that it is a Church, while their critics are arguing whether it is a Church in some sense or other may be a matter of definition, but it certainly is a bureaucracy.

Bureaucracies are not exempt from moral judgment, of course. Even a business corporation should acknowledge the obligation of socially responsible behavior. It is legitimate to raise the question in a stockholders' meeting of Polaroid whether its photographic equipment will be used to produce identity cards in South Africa. But that does not mean that a stockholders' meeting of General Motors is the plausible place to debate a resolution condemning the Nestle Company for encouraging mothers in the Third World to bottle-feed their babies instead of nursing them.

The tensions between those who offer general resolutions in denominational meetings and those who oppose their introduction becomes especially troublesome when it discloses a divergence of views between clergy and laity, or at least a significant segment of the laity. The clergy may well feel frustrated if it appears that people in the pews are not responding as they should to moral leadership. That is because the clergy are more likely to operate from ecclesiastical presuppositions, while the lay persons in question live their lives, very often, within corporate structures and are sensitive to the requirements of bureaucratic organization. So the clergy will be among the first to enlist when the advocates of some protest or other decide to organize a demonstration, and go off to City Hall or the State House to picket, carry banners, and chant slogans. But those who think of the General Assembly as a meeting of the stockholders will not carry banners and chant slogans. That is not how their own corporations carry on their affairs. If the President of American Tel & Tel wants to get something done, he doesn't demonstrate outside the office of the person he wishes to influence. He is accustomed to a different, and in his own experience a more effective, way of attaining his ends.

A basic rule of behavior for a bureaucracy is to avoid courses of action that will injure the bureaucracy itself and perhaps lead to self-destruction. Self-protection is the rule, and the bottom line is survival. A different rule of behavior is the ultimate, though not necessarily the proximate, requirement of religion. He that loseth his life shall find it. There are times when churches and denominations must ask themselves how much they should compromise for the sake of survival, at the expense of moral integrity. Wherever there is a denominational bureaucracy, this ambiguity, this tension is built into the structure.

I must admit that I look back with some nostalgia to an earlier day, when our forebears were very careful to organize their voluntary societies for the administration of affairs separately from their denominational structures. There was a very strong sense at that time that bureaucracies should limit their activities very rigorously to the stated purposes for which they were formed. Yet it was a constant struggle to maintain the boundaries. The temptation was always there for the promoters of one cause to try to take advantage of the established strength of a society already organized for a different one. And so the American Anti-Slavery Society split over the issue of women's rights; while Samuel Joseph May excoriated the Unitarian Association for not becoming an antislavery society also.

We can't go back to that earlier day. But does that mean that there are no alternatives to the present conflicts in our denominations between the demands of religious witness and commitment, and the requirements of the bureaucracies we so often criticize but cannot do without?

Tensions exist among us for a number of reasons, not all of which are structural. But to the extent that our organizational structure itself produces tension and frustration, we are not without recourse. We could do better.

7

Social Cohesion and the Uses of the Past

Address at conference of
Unitarian Universalist ministers,
Cambridge, Massachusetts, February, 1964

As liberals, we have a curiously ambivalent attitude towards the past, and indeed towards history in general. We like to insist that our faces must be set towards the future. New times bring new customs, we assert; we must not be bound by the confining hand of tradition, but must be alert to adjust to new situations, and to be hospitable to new ideas. We must be willing to break new ground, to experiment freshly, to explore new frontiers of the spirit, to cast aside the old when it no longer satisfies our needs. Remember some of the hymns we sing:

> God send us men whose aim 'twill be
> Not to defend some ancient creed
> But to live out the laws of Right
> In every thought and word and deed.

Of course, *Hymns of the Spirit* also contains "Faith of our fathers, living still"; but the editors carefully relegated it to the special section at the back of the book made up of hymns that they wanted to drop but didn't quite dare to do so.

Paradoxically, when we adopt this attitude of rejection of tradition, we are being quite conventionally traditional; for this antihistorical attitude itself has a history. We have been much marked by the influence of the Enlightenment of the eighteenth century, with its faith that reason can create a fair new world, if only the follies, superstitions, and injustices of ancient creeds and inherited institutions could be cast aside. A story is told of the historian Gibbon, who was traveling on the continent and passed through a town that lay in the shadow of one of the great medieval Gothic cathedrals. He is supposed to have remarked: "I darted a glance at the stately monument of superstition,"—a comment which, I submit, is hardly the final word of sophisticated judgment on the cathedrals of Amiens and Chartres. This attitude of the Enlightenment was reinforced in our tradition, though the basis for it was radically altered, by the Transcendentalists who sought to remind us of the continuing and present availability of whatever spiritual resources we have relied on throughout all time. "Acquaint thyself at first hand with deity," Emerson admonished his hearers; and when he turned to the writings of previous generations and ransacked the riches of the past, he did so with an incorrigibly unhistorical attitude towards history.

A kind of rejection of the past is therefore a very traditional part of our collective mentality; and it is reinforced today especially by the presence of the "comeouter" in considerable numbers among us. The comeouter's emancipation from a more orthodox background often carries over into the new allegiance in the form of a distaste for anything that is suspected of being traditional. The vocabulary of religious discourse, the forms of religious worship, the focus of religious emotions, the categories of religious thought—all these for the comeouter must be purged of anything reminiscent of that which has been abandoned. It often takes time to realize that the undiscriminating rejection of the past is a form of bondage to it, quite as much as the undiscriminating acceptance of it is. But this kind of person is not uncommon among us today, as we all doubtless know from first-hand experience.

Yet at the same time that we insist that our faces must be set towards the future, we display an extraordinary pride of ancestry; and this fact points to the other part of our ambivalence towards the past. What publicity pamphlet issuing from 25 Beacon Street does not remind us of the number of Unitarians in the Hall of Fame, or to be found in the beadroll of the great literary figures of the New England renaissance? This became a standard gambit of Unitarian publicity about two generations ago; today the only difference is that Dorothea Dix has been asked to move over to make room for Clara Barton, and William Ellery Channing suddenly finds the name of Hosea Ballou or John Murray coupled with his, in a sort of *ex post facto* right hand of fellowship.

As one encounters the familiar lists of the great names of bygone days and sees the use made of them for publicity purposes, one wonders whether any religious denomination is guilty of more blatant idolatry of the past. With all our insistence on looking to the future, we actually spend a good deal of time encouraging ancestor worship. Our enthusiasm for this undertaking borders at times on the indecent: it strikes me as scandalous the way we are sometimes found laying claim to people who were never associated with either a Unitarian or Universalist church and did no more than say a good word for religious freedom. When we erroneously lay claim to present-day members of the United States Senate, as happened recently, it was possible for the Senator to set the record straight. But when we do the same for some worthy long since under the sod, the myth is perpetuated from one publicity pamphlet to the next. We have found an effective advertising slogan to be: "Are you a Unitarian without knowing it?" A lot of so-called Unitarians of the past belong in the same category: we have collected a number of waifs and strays of the left wing of the Reformation, and a number of anti-ecclesiastical rationalists like Tom Paine and Thomas Jefferson, who are now safely ranked among our number, since they are dead and cannot protest.

It is sometimes a temptation, in certain quarters at least, to argue that there are really two kinds of Unitarians or Universalists. There are those—typically in New England—who are hoary with the accumulated moss of the centuries, who still think that what was good enough for Channing is good enough for them, for whom Unitarianism or Universalism is a kind of family heirloom to be handed down from generation to generation along with the rose medallion tea set. Then on the other hand there are those—who presumably breathe the freer air west of the Hudson, or is it the Mississippi—who are so busy creating the future that they have no time for the veneration of their ancestors.

Making due allowance for the distortions that always creep in when we play around with typologies, I am inclined to agree that both kinds of religious liberals do exist. But my own hunch is that there is a lot less to this business of geographical differences than some people would like to suppose. Channing has some churches named for him near Boston, to be sure, and a statue in the Boston Public Gardens. But then Starr King has a mountain in Yosemite, a theological school in Berkeley, and a statue of his own in Golden Gate Park. Massachusetts does not have much to teach California about the canonization of dead worthies.

You understand, of course, that I regard it as a sound instinct, as well as an inescapable part of human nature, that we should cultivate an acquaintanceship with our ancestors. I am glad that the Starr King School has Earl Morse Wilbur's typewriter on display in a glass case, where it can be venerated as in a very real sense a relic of a saint. I only wish that Harvard had the pen with which Ralph Waldo Emerson composed the Divinity School Address in 1838. Such tangible mementoes perform a necessary service in keeping alive our common memories.

Our history does matter to us, even though its chief value may not be the use that can be made of it for purposes of promotion and publicity. Certainly one of the most important functions that a sense of the past plays in the life of any group is to serve as a cement to bind together various social elements that would otherwise become fragmented and dispersed. If there is any point at all in having a liberal movement in religion that is sufficiently united to accomplish anything, we cannot afford to overlook the role of tradition in sustaining cohesive sentiment.

When we ask ourselves: What is it that unites Unitarians and Universalists? How do we explain the irrational fact that a Universalist in Portland, Maine, feels some genuine sense of relatedness to an unknown Unitarian in Portland, Oregon? Our first impulse is to try to define the nature of that cohesion in terms of the acceptance of a common ideology. We may not subscribe to a common creed, we admit; but we share common attitudes and even accept common doctrines and practices. Yet what doctrine or doctrinal complex is it that is peculiarly ours? Is it a denial of the doctrine of the Trinity? That does not win us financial support from Moslems or Jews. Is it congregational polity? If so, the Park Street Church should have a lot in common with us. Is it that we have common hopes for a future world of human kinship? I venture to say that our dreams in similar form are shared with more religiously concerned people outside our denomination than there are people within the fold. It may be possible for us to define in terms of ideology a consensus that we share; but such an exercise in definition does not explain our groupiness as a sociological entity.

We do share attitudes and doctrines of the sort just mentioned; but our distinctiveness and our cohesion are to be found not in the faith we profess, but in the fact that we profess it in the context of a particular historical tradition which belongs to us and no one else. We do not simply believe in the Free Mind as a philosophical principle; we believe in it as a concern that we share with men like Channing and Starr King, who are still in some sense present with us today. There are devoted friends of freedom in many denominations; but it is only in ours that Channing's lines beginning: "I call that mind free . . . " can operate on those levels of our being where we are stirred to creative joint endeavor.

What the past does is to supply common symbols, by which communication within a group may be facilitated. It supplies the group with what may be termed a "community of discourse," both linguistic and symbolic, by which its members communicate their dreams and visions to one another, and enlist one another's involvement in common action. This communication may be rational and verbal, as when we state as precisely as we can what seems to us most precious and worthwhile, and most deserving of our common devotion. But this communication can also proceed by way of allusion instead of precise definition. It may rely on symbols rather than words; for the community of discourse of which we speak includes many levels, some of them inaccessible to speech.

How this can operate effectively may be illustrated by an episode at May Meetings a dozen or more years ago. One of our younger ministers, animated by very deep idealism, offered a motion to the effect that the financial aid of the Association should be denied to any member church that did not live up to the moral standards of the Association at large on an issue then being agitated. As I recall, it was the question of racial segregation that was under discussion. One could see delegates getting all set to line up at the microphones to take off on an hour or two of excited and inconclusive discussion of the kind that has become characteristic of such occasions.

Frederick Eliot did not often allow himself to get drawn into such hassles; but on this occasion he rose quickly and gained recognition from the Chair. I cannot reproduce his exact words, but the tenor of them remains vivid in my mind. "Many of you will recall," he said,

> that this same question has been discussed among us before in a somewhat different form. The question is whether the financial resources of the Association shall be used to coerce one of our churches, even when the majority of our delegates believe that the issues are clear and should admit of one answer. This issue arose during World War I, when the Board of Directors of the Association voted that no assistance should be given to any church whose minister was not a firm supporter of the Allied war effort. A number of our ministers were forced from their pulpits in consequence; some who conscientiously held pacifist views felt that the only honorable thing for them to do was to withdraw from our ministry. Two decades later we repented of that act, at the urging of Henry W. Pinkham, and passed a resolution of regret for our error. I believe we should not repeat today the mistake made in 1917.

I repeat, these are not Frederick Eliot's exact words; but I think they are true to the intent of his remarks. I remembered

Henry Pinkham as an old man, bent over by the infirmities of age; and I had been told more than once of the loss to our cause because John Haynes Holmes had withdrawn from our fellowship. The resolution that had been passed was called the Pinkham Resolution. But the real symbol that Dr. Eliot's remarks brought freshly to the minds of those present at that session was Henry Pinkham himself, his hair white, his hands shaking, his voice hoarse but arresting because of its obvious sincerity, pleading with his fellow Unitarians almost with his dying breath, to wipe away a stain from their record of which John Haynes Holmes and he himself had been the victims.

The response to Frederick Eliot's brief speech was immediate. The young minister who had made the motion spoke up at once. "Of course," he said; "I remember; I should have thought of that. I withdraw the motion."

Because these men, together with many of the delegates present, shared common memories, the question was disposed of in less than five minutes without a dissenting voice being raised. Had it been necessary to argue the matter out at the level of rational debate, exploring all the pros and cons, there would doubtless have been a protracted argument, frayed tempers, intemperate remarks, and an uncertain outcome. By using the symbols of communication that were peculiar to that group, and drawn from its collective memory, instead of the less pointed vocabulary of general debate, Dr. Eliot not only accomplished his purpose, but did it with efficiency and dispatch, at the same time protecting the social cohesion of the group. Fortunately, there were symbols from the past he could evoke; equally fortunately, the tradition to which he was appealing was a sound and healthy one.

One may plausibly argue that factors such as these are essential to the survival of all social groups. There have to be, in other words, communities of memory as well as of hope. It is surely no accident that the Jews, who have retained their identity through the centuries, despite bondage in Egypt, exile in Babylon, persecution in the ghetto, and attempted extermination in the concentration camp—who have even retained their identity in the open society of the United States—have always had a strong sense of a covenant between God and their fathers, which must be freshly brought to mind in common worship, especially on ceremonial occasions like Passover and Hannukah. Without the historic basis for these celebrations, their moral content would long since have been diluted or dispersed. No one can genuinely enter into a Hannukah celebration unless some way is found to identify with the group memories on which it is based.

Thus far, my plea has been for a recognition of the legitimacy of apologetic history. By "apologetic history" I mean the sympathetic exploration and retelling of the history of a group with a view to reinforcing its social cohesion. In making such a plea, I obviously run certain professional risks, since most historians regard apologetic history as a species of corruption to be avoided at all costs. They are trained to respect certain canons of objectivity; and a historian who so identifies with the group whose history is being examined as to become to any degree an apologist for it will quickly compromise his or her professional reputation. The church historian is in a particularly vulnerable position, because much of the literature in the field, covering the whole range of groupings from denominations down to the local parish, is apologetic in the worst sense. Furthermore, some church historians have been known to argue on theological grounds that only a committed Christian can write the history of the Church—a position which, I hasten to state, is not mine at all. To defend the apologetic use of church history, then, is not the obvious way to heal the breach between the church historian and the so-called secular historian.

One might reply that to stand outside a group rather than to observe it from within does not assure objectivity. The observer from without can be just as biased as anyone else. The late Perry Miller, when I first knew him, was sometimes heard to declare that he joined no church lest membership distort his view of the religious scene he sought to examine and appraise. Perhaps he sincerely thought so then. But that did not prevent him, as time went on, from cultivating the luxuriant growth of prejudices that readers of his later books have to guard against the more vigilantly because he continued to maintain the fiction of objectivity. To my mind it is almost axiomatic that any historian who *claims* to be objective is in danger of becoming the victim of hidden prejudices. The only safe course for the historian is to acknowledge at the outset that there is an apologetic thrust in much writing of history, so as to confront openly and frankly his or her own inevitable biases. The situation is comparable to that of the psychoanalyst, who must first undergo analysis before engaging in therapy.

There is no necessary reason why the apologetic concerns that motivate writers of denominational history should corrupt their integrity as historians, or vitiate their work. There is no good reason, that is, provided they have been trained to avoid certain obvious pitfalls that lie along their path. The bad reputation that denominational and parish historians have long had stems from the fact that most of them have been written by people who have not been trained to avoid the characteristic faults of this kind of historical writing, not because those faults are inherently unavoidable.

Three such characteristic faults immediately come to mind. In the first place, even when the apologetic historian strives to tell the truth the temptation remains not to tell the whole truth. Episodes which do not reflect credit on the group in question are likely to be skirted or ignored. Recently I had occasion to read a new history of the Episcopal diocese of Connecticut, covering the whole period from colonial times to the present. As historians are well aware, in the period before the Civil War the Episcopal church dealt with the moral issues of slavery and abolition by saying as little as possible. There were reasons, doubtless more sociological than theological, for this silence. There were also important consequences of it, some of them very happy consequences so far as the ability of the church to meet the problems of reconstruction after the war was concerned. Yet by present-day standards, the Episcopal church was guilty of evasion when confronted by the most significant moral issue of that day; and some modern Episcopalian historians have not hesitated to say so quite bluntly. But in 500 pages of the history of the diocese of Connecticut just mentioned, you will find a total of three paragraphs devoted to the matter.

In the second place, when conflict between competing groups

is involved, the apologetic historian finds it hard even to present the case for the opposition, let alone to consider whether it is in any measure justified. In this connection, one aspect of the Unitarian Controversy, as treated by Unitarian historians, comes to mind. As we all know, the disposition of the property of churches that were split by the controversy was governed in Massachusetts by the decision in Baker *v*. Fales, in 1820. The practical consequence of this case, commonly known as the Dedham Case, was that a considerable amount of property, which the orthodox believed was rightfully theirs, was adjudged to belong to the liberals. There were a few instances where the shoe was on the other foot; but there is little reason to doubt that the liberals did not come out second best in this transaction. The orthodox immediately set up the cry: "We wuz robbed"; and though the wounds finally healed, the scars remain, and anyone who wants to probe will discover that it is still possible to reopen old sores, even after 150 years.

Unitarian historians have been quite scrupulously objective in stating the facts of the Dedham Case; they have been willing to acknowledge that the result was financially advantageous to the liberals, and they have not tried to conceal the fact that the judge who wrote the decision was a Unitarian. But they have not taken seriously the complaint of the orthodox that the decision was grounded on a faulty reading of New England ecclesiastical history and practices. One can easily get the impression from them that the orthodox were upset because they lost the case. It is easy to understand that a person who loses out on a legal decision will not be happy about it; but after all, the courts have spoken and the law is the law. But in this particular case it is the more understandable that Congregationalists should respond with some asperity because at just the same time, the Plan of Union with the Presbyterians in western New York state was resulting in the subversion of dozens of Congregational churches and their transformation into Presbyterian ones. "They have milked our Congregational cows," one Congregationalist complained, "but have made nothing but Presbyterian butter and cheese." No sooner did the Unitarians in Massachusetts finish stealing their money, than the Presbyterians in New York began stealing whole churches. No wonder the Congregationalist have never gotten over it.

I happen to be one who believes that, in the Dedham Case, the orthodox position was a much stronger one than Unitarian historians have ever let on. I might even go so far as to assert that the decision in the case was dead wrong. This does not mean that I am agitating to reopen the question as the present ownership of the property in question. The legal doctrine of *res judicata* would seem to apply; and that Latin term when translated into English means: Don't reopen old sores. All I am arguing is that even the Unitarian historian has an obligation to try to understand why the Congregationalists were so upset.

The third pitfall of the apologetic historian is a consequence of the fact that the historian is presumably committed to particular goals or objectives for the group, and there is a tendency to show that the image of the group's future is sustained by its past. What it is hoped the group may achieve has to be seen as an appropriate culmination of its previous development, even if that means a very selective reading of the past. A skillful apologist can do all sorts of weird and wonderful things with the historical record when seized with this particular fit. The writing of Unitarian history itself has suffered a good deal from this kind of distortion. Sometime in the latter part of the last century, the canonization of Emerson and Parker was completed, and the convention established that they represent the Great Tradition of American Unitarian history. The literary eminence of Emerson helped to bring about this outcome; but another influential factor may have been the work of Octavius Brooks Frothingham, who contributed as much through his patronizing account of his own father in *Boston Unitarianism* as by his book on *Transcendentalism in New England.*

Frothingham was of course not a bystander in the conflicts and tensions in Unitarianism that convulsed the denomination in the decades following the Civil War. He was one of the leading spirits in the Free Religious Association, which played the same role vis à vis institutional and conservative Unitarianism in the 1870s and 1880s that Transcendentalism had a generation earlier. Small wonder that for him it is Emerson and Parker who represent the main line of development, and that little recognition is given to the contributions of those who disagreed with them. Our own generation is engaged in the old familiar process of revisionist historical writing; it is no longer regarded as improper to say a good word for Andrews Norton, Henry Ware, Jr., Henry W. Bellows, or a whole host of others who have long been dismissed as stuffed shirts. I suppose, however, that the historical conventions of an earlier generation will linger on for a long time in our publicity handouts and religious education curricula materials, since it takes time for subtle revolutions in historical scholarship to make their influence felt.

Perhaps the only way for the apologetic historian to guard against the several pitfalls we have reviewed is to write as though the audience were made up exclusively of secular historians with no stake whatsoever in the enterprise he or she has so much at heart. They are the ones to be convinced that the treatment of the group is not unduly colored by the historian's own legitimate loyalties. And then, if the historian who is an outsider will assume that a picture must be presented that is at least recognizable by the insiders, even if they are made uncomfortable by it, we may guard against the opposite kind of bias.

This discussion of the uses and abuses of apologetic history has admittedly been colored by many professional concerns, of chief consequence for practicing historians. Yet I think there are implications of significance to all among us who are concerned with sustaining the kind of cohesion that will enable us to make an impact on the life of our times. I think it is of the first importance for us to understand the legitimate role of apologetic history, so that we may use our history wisely.

I trust it is clear that I am not saying that the good old days were better than today, or that the precedents of the past are binding upon us. New occasions do teach new duties. Change is the law of life, and social institutions that do not learn how to adjust to new times and altered circumstances have chosen the pathway to extinction. But there is more than one way of committing suicide. The social organism that refuses to recognize that change is inevitable will atrophy. On the other hand, the social organism that, in the attempt to adjust, fails to respect its own nature, will disintegrate. It is the responsibility of the historian, understanding both the value and dangers of apologetic history, to use it so that the social group may discover how to make the inevitable renewal of life come about as the fulfillment rather than the repudiation of the past.

8

Unitarian Universalist History
in the
Church School Curriculum

◆

Address at a Religious Education Conference,
Crane Theological School,
October 14, 1963

Unitarian Universalists have long had an ambivalent attitude toward the past, never being sure whether to reject or embrace it. On the one hand, we think of ourselves as emancipated from the bondage and burden of traditional Christian dogma. We have discarded the inherited vocabulary of theology—God, sin, atonement, justification—or remythologized it so that it bears only a remote resemblance to its former meanings. The conventional focus of religious emotions in the life and death of Jesus Christ has lost much of its power. Now we are free to look to the future, without regret for what has been discarded, and to explore new horizons of religious insight and truth. With eager voices, we sing:

> Age after age we rise,
> 'Neath the eternal skies,
> Into the light from the shadowed past.

Yet at the same time, we display an extraordinary pride of ancestry, even if it is sometimes necessary to stretch a point to do so. Perhaps we no longer stress, as Universalists were once wont to do, that Origen in the third century was a Universalist, as though there were some continuous tradition linking him to John Murray, to give Universalism the prestige of ancient lineage. But Unitarians still assume a kinship with Michael Servetus in the sixteenth century, as though his rejection of the Nicean version of the doctrine of the Trinity anticipated a very different antitrinitarianism in the eighteenth century. We name churches for Thomas Jefferson and Ralph Waldo Emerson, though neither had a concept of religion that recognized any need for churches and other religious institutions. We invoke the shades of Channing, Emerson, and Parker—and Hosea Ballou, too—on ceremonial occasions, and use quotations from Emerson's Divinity School Address in our services.

In short, we seem unable to decide whether the past is best forgotten or glorified—to be cast aside as irrelevant or to be cherished. Both of these attitudes are fraught with danger. It is easy to brag about our ancestors; it is not so easy to make an equivalent contribution to cultural life today. We must stand or fall by our own achievement, not by the recollection of theirs; if we have minimal impact on our own times, we cannot compensate by clinging to the comforting thought that the influence of our leaders in an earlier time extended beyond their own denomination. Yet much is lost if we allow a rich inheritance to fall into oblivion, or worse, allow ourselves to be maneuvered into a repudiation of it.

Our achievement is sustained by the traditions we inherit, and any distinction we may win for ourselves is enriched to the extent that it can be regarded as a fulfillment of the hopes and dreams of our ancestors. Our problem as liberals is to understand the past and accept it without being enslaved by it; to respect it even as we face the future; to use it, not as a refuge from the problems of today, but as a spiritual resource that enables us to grapple with them.

Our ambivalent attitude towards our own history reappears when we concern ourselves with the shaping of attitudes of our children, specifically with the place of Unitarian and Universalist history in our church school curricula. Whether it should be taught, and why, are questions to which we find no generally accepted and unambiguous answers. If we are ambivalent in our attitude towards history, it is not surprising that we don't know what to do about it in our church school programs.

In general, the position seems to be that it is probably a good thing for the kids to hear about Channing and Ballou before they quit Sunday school to join the church or go off to college. So the leader for the high-school age group looks around to find something about a subject on which his or her ideas are vague and information is hazy, and discovers that useable material is hard to find. If the leader is in one of the Universalist churches, the result is a couple of hastily prepared summaries of the lives of Murray and Ballou. Or if the church is Unitarian in origin, the talks equally hastily prepared are on Channing, Emerson, and Parker. Or perhaps the Unitarian starts to read Earl Morse Wilbur's two volumes, gets bogged down in Transylvania or Poland in the sixteenth century, and decides to postpone the whole business until next year.

The situation is clearly unsatisfactory, and not all the fault lies with directors and teachers of our church schools. I won't even say the fault lies with the staff of the Department of Education at 25 Beacon Street. Perhaps the fault lies with the historians among us; if so, I prefer not to publicize the fact. Perhaps fault is so diffused among us that we are all to blame in some measure for not having a wiser understanding of the uses of history, which could then be translated into imperatives and guides for those responsible for curriculum materials.

Why does our history matter to us? I think it does matter, and I do not think its chief value is publicity and promotion. I would like to suggest four uses of history, which may be outlined in general terms, applicable to groups of various sorts, but with clear implications for our own situation.

The first use of history is the support it can give to social cohesion. Illustrations of this principle are legion. When blacks come to group consciousness and seek to exert influence and exercise power consonant with their strength, there is immediately a concern for black history and a demand that it be taught. When the women's movement emerged, a major component of women's studies in universities was women's history. A sense of a common past is equally important in unifying religious groups. Let a Methodist change denominations and become a Unitarian Universalist, and very soon he or she will discover the need to become acquainted with a new set of ancestors. John Wesley will no longer be appealed to; Channing, Emerson, and Hosea Ballou will become common points of reference and it will be necessary to learn about them.

The second use of history is closely related to the first: it provides us with many of our symbols of communication. At the purely intellectual level, there are concepts drawn from the past that we can use as a sort of shorthand, as when we may speak of an "Augustinian strain of piety" (as Perry Miller does in *The New England Mind*), or a "Lockean concept of human nature." But on more of a gut level, there can be an appeal to common experience, or experience shared vicariously, as when a reference to the Holocaust can communicate a whole range of sensibilities to Jews, whether or not they themselves or their families were involved.

The third use of history is that it supplies role models for later generations. Historical figures who fascinate us exert a subtle influence on our behavior. There have been many throughout the generations who, like Thomas à Kempis, have sought to imitate Christ; the example of Socrates has been in the mind of many a teacher. There is always the risk of evil models: consider the imitation of Hitler by Neo-Nazis. But we do need sound models, and Jesus cannot do everything for us. The Catholic Church wisely canonizes a variety of saints, and not all are of one mold. The gentleness of St. Francis of Assisi will appeal to some, the militance of St. Ignatius of Loyola to others. Thomas Aquinas is for the philosophically inclined; John of the Cross is for mystics.

We need models from our own tradition as well as from the larger experience of humankind; and we have them, too, if we will only recognize our riches. Usually, however, we limit ourselves to Emerson as the representative of spiritual religion and Theodore Parker as a voice for social reform. We overlook a whole range of other kinds of excellence. We have great churchmen in Henry W. Bellows and Frederick May Eliot; exceptionally gifted parish ministers in Henry Ware, Jr., Ezra Stiles Gannett, and many others who may not now be remembered outside the places where they served; great preachers in

Channing and John Haynes Holmes; scholars with a religious commitment to the search for truth, such as Andrews Norton; shapers of public opinion like Charles W. Eliot, remembered as much for his integrity of character as for educational leadership; humanitarian reformers like Dorothea Dix and Clara Barton; a transformer of educational methods in Sophia L. Fahs; servants of their communities as well as of their own flocks, like William Greenleaf Eliot. No one of these can contribute all we need; they complement each other. It seems especially important to recover the role models appropriate for those who must take responsibility for the health of religious institutions, whether local or denominational.

The fourth use of history is as an aid to self-understanding. It helps us to know better who we are. No inventory of attitudes and values of Unitarian Universalists at any given moment will tell what they really stand for. Nor can one tell simply by watching them argue current issues. It is necessary to see what concerns they have persistently addressed, what patterns of thought and behavior recur repeatedly, what continuous lines are drawn, down through the decades. It tells us something to note that at Syracuse in 1959 the relationship of Unitarians and Universalists to the Christian tradition was debated in connection with the constitution of the proposed Unitarian Universalist Association. It tells us much more to recall that the same issue was debated in the same place in 1865 in connection with the constitution of the proposed National Conference of Unitarian Churches.

A consciousness of a common past is a force that strengthens loyalties to the group. The reason we regard it as important for our children to have an historical awareness is to make them good Unitarian Universalists. Let us make no bones about it. We teach our history so that children will have such a sense of belonging and knowing who they are that when they grow up there is a chance that they will remain Unitarian Universalists, and not become Episcopalians or Presbyterians. We will not necessarily succeed in making them all lifelong churchgoers, though some of them may turn out that way; but they will know which church it is they are not going to on Sunday.

Is this not indoctrination? Will not children revolt against it? Shouldn't we allow them the freedom to choose for themselves? These arguments are familiar; the replies should be equally so. The transmission of culture from one generation to the next is essential, and parents and teachers are engaged in it every day. We begin talking to our children the day they are born. Language is a transmitter of culture, and some languages are better than others for particular purposes. But we do not refuse to talk English to our children for fear of indoctrinating them; we do not suggest that they should wait until they are of age to learn to speak because Japanese might turn out to be of more use to them. We inexorably form their taste in diet, recreation, vocational expectations, and all sorts of other human concerns, without worrying whether we are denying them an opportunity to choose for themselves.

The supposition that religion should be an exception is a misapplication of one of the insights of our Transcendentalist forebears: that the life of religion must be freshly recreated in the souls of each successive generation. It does not follow, however, that what Emerson termed the "religious sentiment" in each individual soul can create its own form of expression in isolation from the cultural inheritance. The child who grows up without the stimulus of others speaking to it in whatever is the conventional language of that time and place is linguistically and culturally aborted. The child who grows up without some religious indoctrination to assimilate and do battle with remains religiously unsophisticated.

How, then, do we go about the transmission of our religious inheritance? Much of it may take place in the home; but there is still much for the church to do, and which it may be able to do better.

The initial reaction of most of us would be to set aside time for part of the curriculum to be devoted to Unitarian Universalist history, and to ask the curriculum development people to supply curriculum materials. Possibly something may be accomplished this way, but I am skeptical—and certainly skeptical of the notion that one should wait as long to begin instruction as is implied by such a procedure. High-school age is much too late, not only because school and social pressures make it hard to hold a class together. But why wait that long? What is called for is for children to develop a sense of meaningful linkages with the past, and that is something other than mastering a systematic survey of church history.

With younger ages, to foster group loyalties, one should think primarily in terms of the local church, not of the wider fellowship of Unitarian Universalist churches. Do a good job at that level, and the basis is laid for wider loyalties to develop as the child grows and horizons expand. It is therefore the history and traditions of the local church that should somehow or other get into the minds and hearts of the primary class group—and the five-year olds, and the four-year olds.

Our adult encounters with history courses make it difficult for us—for historians in particular—to see the alternatives. The chief problem for the historian is a professional bias in favor of the presentation of historical materials in orderly, systematic, usually chronological form. We must get over this prejudice, and be willing to establish linkages with the past in any order, however haphazard, relying on the children's increasing maturity to produce in due course some degree of coherence and orderliness. We must resort to the immediate experiences of children, with alertness to use them to develop an historical awareness. In discussing this problem, I propose to use a few illustrations, drawing directly on my own experience in the church in Cambridge. The principles involved can be translated into the special case of any local community.

The first device is to make use of the experience of concrete material objects. The Church School in Cambridge meets for a service of worship in the Crothers Chapel. Who was Dr. Crothers? There is a commemorative tablet on the wall, and his picture in the next room. That may be enough to begin with, for the youngest children, but more can be built on it later. Then there is the meetinghouse—the fifth meetinghouse of the parish. Where were the others and what did they look like? Why were Harvard Commencements held in this building and why was Emerson's Phi Beta Kappa address on the American Scholar delivered here?

What do such events say about the relationship between the church and the university? Once upon a time, the city fire alarm involved striking the bell in the tower; what does that suggest about the relationship between the parish and the town? The building has some curious anomalies of architecture; how did these come about? What happened to some of the crockets and finials of the Gothic style of architecture that once adorned the exterior of the building, as we see in old photographs? A tablet in the vestibule lists the names of ministers for 350 years; what do the names Shepard, Brattle, Appleton, and Hilliard suggest? From time to time a silver christening basin, the gift of the Reverend William Brattle, is brought from the Art Museum. Who was he? Where did he get it? And why did he give it to the church?

The second device is the experience of storytelling. In dealing with concrete historical objects, the association of an artifact with an historical person can often be made vivid by the use of anecdote. In the case of Dr. Crothers, there is the story of his first visit to the Unitarian May Meetings, when he decided to take the boat to Nantasket Beach instead of going to the sessions. Or the story of his changing his clothes in the cab between the wedding at which he had officiated and the North Station, where he had only just enough time to catch the train to Chocorua. But some anecdotes or stories may be prior to or independent of any physical relic. President Eliot might be used as an example of churchmanship, or integrity, or a relationship between religion and higher learning. There are plenty of anecdotes to bring his memory to life again: his response to the child who was crying because his playmates made fun of a physical handicap; his concern for the budget of the University, which led him to go around turning down the gas in the President's house; his taking in of the Crothers family in time of illness; his response to the Freshman who aroused him in the middle of the night to tell him that it had been revealed to him (the student) that he (President Eliot) was about to accept the Lord Jesus Christ as his personal savior; even Eliot's insistence—some called it stubbornness—that if the meetinghouse was to be rebuilt, the architecture should be brick colonial, not stone Gothic. In our families we tell stories of this kind to our children and they pass them on to theirs. A church should be a sort of family, also.

The third device is the experience of ritual observances. The service of worship is the most obvious ritualistic exercise. For some churches, the liturgy plays an enormous part in promoting group cohesion, as, for example, the use of the prayer book in Episcopal churches—or the use of the prayer book at King's Chapel. We encounter two problems here. The first is that we have no fixed form of worship generally accepted throughout our churches; hence in a local situation there is no respect for any particular form. The second problem is akin to the first: that there are many Unitarian Universalists who think a service of worship should be a spontaneous happening without antecedents. So, as religious education directors come and go, they alter the children's worship service at will. Yet is there not a place in the service of worship for the prayer Dr. Crothers wrote especially for children, used both for its continuing significance and its linkage with the past?

Ritual observances, to be sure, are not confined to the order of Sunday worship. An Easter flower in a flower pot (years ago it was always a geranium), a mitten tree, a flaming chalice, flower communion—these can have an historical as well as an aesthetic and a religiously symbolic meaning, and be enriched thereby.

This is perhaps enough to illustrate that a sense of relatedness to the past is part of the cement of social cohesion; that it can develop out of experience in haphazard, disconnected fashion, and be gradually reshaped into a respectably orderly whole as children grow older; and that it begins with what is close at hand, in the local traditions and lore of a given parish church, and it gradually widens its horizons so as to relate the local church to the denomination, and beyond, to the religious experience of humankind.

This is a job to be thought out in its own terms for each church. There are no published materials from 25 Beacon Street to put in the hands of the teacher. Success will depend on the attitude of parents and teachers much more than it does on the historical resources of a given church; that is to say, historically-minded teachers are needed, not a church with a long historical tradition and famous names on its roster of ministers. But this foundation will make it possible at the upper age levels to introduce historical materials with greater sophistication and depth, in place of the shallow surveys that otherwise seem to be all that is available.

9

The Mirror of History

Address at the Commencement Exercises of the
Meadville Theological School of Lombard College,
June 4, 1968

"Our age is retrospective," declared Emerson in 1836. "It builds
the sepulchres of the fathers. It writes biographies, histories, and
criticism. The foregoing generations beheld God and nature face
to face; we, through their eyes." But Emerson was not content to
have it so. His was a plea for poetry and philosophy "of insight
and not of tradition"; and a religion of immediate, present
experience, not the history of a past revelation. Why should we
"grope among the dry bones of the past," he asked, "or put the
living generation into masquerade out of its faded wardrobe?"

Unitarians and Universalists have taken these injunctions
very much to heart; they have long been part of our unques-
tioned and traditional liberal dogma. One consequence has been
to place on the historians among us a special burden of account-
ing for themselves and justifying the relevance of their professional concerns. It may be assumed that the historian will be
found groping among the dry bones of the past. How does that
qualify him to say anything of value to those who, if they have
learned nothing else, have surely learned that the year 2000 will
be one in which most of the landmarks of today will have been
washed away? We shall need new institutional forms, new
patterns of social organization, and new categories of thought if
we are to handle the problems of a new age. What possible

contribution can familiarity with the issues, let us say, of the year 1800 make to a solution of the problems now confronting us?

Yet there seems to be something in us, a part of our common nature as human beings, that will not let us leave it at that. Even Unitarians and Universalists have memories and celebrate birthdays; even they invoke the sanction of the dead—Unitarians most often Channing, Emerson, and Parker; Universalists, John Murray and Hosea Ballou. Even religious liberals, as contemporary minded as they conceive themselves to be, sometimes discover an obscure urge to write booklets of parish history, or find themselves celebrating the 400th anniversary of the Diet of Torda.

We are caught in inconsistencies that we have not yet thought through. We have an intellectual stance, or mind-set, that does not encourage us to take history seriously; yet we also have inchoate urges to remember and celebrate the triumphs of the human spirit in earlier generations, and define our relationship to them. Our present experience, whether we acknowledge it or not, includes a particular kind of relationship to the past. But if we assume, as Emerson did, that the past is made up of dry bones and a faded wardrobe, how can we do justice to this aspect of our experience of individual and common memory, which we can deny only by denying a part of ourselves? How can we construct a religious view of life that will do justice to the whole range of our present experience, unless we build into it a somewhat more sophisticated understanding of the past, and its protean influence on us than Emerson bequeathed to us?

One of the lessons we learned from Sigmund Freud was that our behavior as individual men and women is often influenced by experiences of infancy and childhood of which we are no longer consciously aware. Traumatic experiences may well be repressed, only to manifest themselves long afterwards in neurotic behavior. The necessary therapy, in classic Freudian theory, involves a process of bringing into consciousness the repressed traumatic experience, so that it may be handled rationally and the neurotic response transformed. The psychoanalyst can assist in the process of self-discovery on the part of patients, not by telling them what is bothering them, but by enabling them to find it out for themselves.

The neurotic behavior of groups may likewise be the result of an inadequate understanding of their own past. Thus a group may develop a conventionalized response to certain situations, only to have its conventional behavior outlast not only the situation that gave rise to it, but even the memory of it. One is entitled to suspect that this may be the case when a group has an image of its own past that is, by omission or distortion, significantly different from the experience of the generations that lived it. The historian may then perform a healing function by assisting the group to relate more realistically to the historical forces that have made it what it is.

Some there may be who will object to such an analogy with a psychoanalytic understanding of neuroses. Perhaps it is enough to argue that a group's image of its own past is such an important part of the ideology with which it tries to make sense of the present that its shaping requires historical practitioners of the highest skill and integrity. The demand for relevance in our thinking is not to be met by denying our sense of the past, rejecting it on the grounds that it might tyrannize over us, or by dismissing it as dry bones and a faded wardrobe, but by using it for increased self-understanding. Those who are fearful lest tradition enslave them should keep in mind that an undiscriminating rejection of the past is as much a form of bondage to it as an undiscriminating reverence for it.

The significance of such considerations came forcibly to mind recently, as I read an address delivered by Frederic Henry Hedge at the annual meeting of the American Unitarian Association in 1882. Two men had just recently died, whom it was his task to memorialize—two men of very different talents and temperaments, but both of them men who had had an enormous impact on the Unitarian body.

One of them was Ralph Waldo Emerson. He was, in Hedge's words, "always a preacher in the higher, universal sense,—a prophet,—the greatest, I think, this country or this age has known." As a preacher, "born and nurtured in our communion, he belongs to us; and . . . as a preacher, he was one of the few in all the ages who in the realm of the spirit have spoken with authority." Emerson was an original observer, Hedge asserted, who, though ridiculed at the outset, had taken his stand on the ground of his own sincerity; and behold, he had created his own public, and formed the taste by which he at last had come to be understood and enjoyed.

The other man whom Hedge memorialized was Henry W. Bellows, whose organizing genius had given to Unitarianism the institutional form and structure that had saved it from dissolution. "He was our Bishop, our Metropolitan," Hedge declared, occupying an office not formally recognized in the denomination, but exercising its functions "by universal consent of the brethren."

> An ecclesiastical Centurion, "set under authority," he said to this man, "Go," and he went; to another, "Come," and he came. He ordered us hither and thither, and we surrendered ourselves to his ordering. One day, he summoned us to New York, and founded the National Conference of Unitarian Churches. Another day, he summoned us to Springfield, and established the Ministers' Institute. These organizations, which we trust will survive him and last as long as our communion shall maintain its specialty and continue a separate fold in universal Christendom, testify of his far-seeing sagacity as well as his far-reaching zeal. They are his monument, had he no other.

Hedge's praise of Bellows for his organizing ability, and his rare skill in the art of democratic leadership, may be matched in the words of others. John White Chadwick, whose theological position was quite different from that of Bellows, said of him that "almost every best thing that has been devised for the last seventeen years within the limits of the Unitarian denomination has taken its initiative from him or to his splendid advocacy owed its practical success." And Cyrus Bartol said, quite simply "Dr. Bellows is the only leader the Unitarian body has ever had."

In 1882, when these two men died, they were equally known and respected among us, though they stood for very different kinds of achievement, and had affected Unitarian development in very different ways. Today, whether we read him or not, we still invoke the shade of Emerson; but who remembers Bellows? Channing, Emerson, and Parker—the inevitable Unitarian Trinity—are familiar names to all of us; we even reprint selections from their writings in paperback using the title: *Three Prophets of Religious Liberalism*. But where is the paperback of complementary selections from Emerson and Bellows, to remind us that we have known in our midst these two contrasting types of greatness? How does it happen that of these two men, both regarded as eminent by their own contemporaries, one is remembered, while the other is forgotten?

Here we have an example of a real discrepancy between our image of the past, and the understanding an earlier generation had of it. Two questions immediately thrust themselves upon us. The first question is simply: How has this come about? What are the reasons for the discrepancy? The second is more elusive: What are some of the consequences of it? Has our failure to understand our own past in this respect affected our ability to deal with our present problems? Does this distorted image of the past provide us with a clue to an understanding of some of our neurotic behavior as a body?

A number of factors might be adduced to explain the disappearance of Bellows from our collective memory. Perhaps the key to them all is that his most creative and innovative work was in the shaping of institutions, into which he built himself so effectively that his continuing influence has become largely anonymous and unrecognized. Emerson's medium of expression was the poetic utterance, which, translated to the printed page, may take on a timeless quality, and provoke fresh response for successive generations of readers. Bellows was an even more prolific writer than Emerson, gifted with a driving masculine style, an extraordinary gift for metaphor, and an exceptional skill in analyzing the social trends and forces of the day. But his writing was instrumental, subordinated to the goal of institutional renovation and fresh creation. He wrote much, without qualifying as a writer by profession. He wrote many letters, without being a Man of Letters. No single writing of his—not even his controversial and widely read address entitled "The Suspense of Faith"—ever quite qualified as a classic formulation of the position for which he stood. In this respect, Emerson has a clear advantage.

Bellows had a charismatic personality, so that his extempore public utterances had an enormous impact on his audiences. But it is not so much in the words he spoke as in the institutions he formed that his lasting influence is to be found. Institutions, however, are not timeless in the way that lyric poems may be. Instead, they develop through time, so that the shaping hand of the first fashioner becomes obscured by later adaptations. Institutional memories are treacherous. How many of us are aware, when we meet in the General Assembly of the Unitarian Universalist Association, that it was Bellows who persuaded the Unitarian body that it needed an assembly in which the churches would be represented by delegates, and that one of the antecedents of our Association is the National Conference he founded in 1865? When we collect money for our annual appeal, how many of us realize that it was Bellows—himself a money-raiser of no mean ability—who first forcefully insisted that Unitarians undergird their common activities with an organized and sustained program of financial support? How many of us, as we attend meetings of our continental body, one year in Denver, the next in Cleveland, remember that it was Bellows, one hundred years ago, who gave voice at a critical juncture in our history to the demand that the movement become truly national lest it atrophy? Emerson once asserted that every institution is the lengthened shadow of a man. We still stand in the shadow of Bellows much more than we realize. But the medium through which his creative vision found expression has lent itself less to an enduring reputation than the one in which Emerson worked.

Thus reasons may be found for the eclipse of Bellow's reputation. But we still must ask ourselves whether it makes any difference after all. Does this particular discrepancy between history as past event, and history as the recollection or reconstruction of past event, have any consequences that need concern us? I think it does.

The history of a social group may be likened to a mirror, in which it finds itself reflected. This may be true in a two-fold sense. For one thing, as we review the record of the past, we are likely to respond with a special sense of self-discovery to aspects of it that illuminate our present-day concerns. Kindred spirits rediscovered in the past sanctify and inspire our own endeavors; and not every generation will canonize the same saints. Who we are, or who we like to think we are, is revealed by the particular ancestors we choose to honor. But we also find our identity, not simply in the patterns of behavior with which we respond to the demands of the present situation, but even more clearly in the continuous line we have drawn through the flux of time. We need the mirror of history to understand ourselves, and we require of the historians that they keep it clear and undistorted.

What that mirror shows us at the moment is a gap wide enough to be unhealthy, between what we are and what we pretend we are. This gap is symbolized by the contrast between Emerson and Bellows. Emerson serves us as a type figure of the fearless rejector of outworn conventions; we like to think that we, too, stand firmly planted on our own individual integrity, developing our own religious faith out of our own insights into spiritual truth. But the final outcome of that position, as Emerson knew full well, was "churches of two, churches of one." Churches are not built on the basis of Emerson's radical individualism. The work of the world is not done that way; on that foundation one can create only the most fleeting kind of fellowship.

There are, of course, Unitarians and Universalists who are resolved to be religious in solitude—with what success or genuine spirituality, I do not presume to say. There are also those among us who would try to make the spiritual harmony, or sense of identity, that sometimes unites two people, the model for religious fellowship generally. But most of us, attracted though we may be to these Emersonian concepts, pay them lip service only, while our actual behavior shows that we remain unpersuaded. To judge by what we do, we believe that the religious life is nourished by companionship and is sustained, especially in time of trial, by institutional forms. A church fair may not be the communion of saints, and a denominational bureaucracy is surely not the kingdom of God. But it may well be that more saints will be recruited from among the workers at church fairs than on the shores of Walden Pond. To the extent that religious institutions—churches, and fellowships, and district offices, and 25 Beacon Street, and the Service Committee, and theological seminaries—represent something we know we must live with and work through, Emerson makes us uneasy without convincing us that he has really found how to get along without them. Perhaps it is a divine discontent that he fosters in us; perhaps on the other hand, he lays the foundation for our most characteristic neurosis.

The type figure we need, if not to replace Emerson then at least to counterbalance him, is Bellows, the churchman, the shaper of a doctrine of institutions in general and of the church in particular. Some, having encountered in Bellows a formulation of Christian doctrine couched in a vocabulary that is much too conservative for our taste today, have hastily assumed that he has nothing to teach us. Consequently, we have done less than justice to his perceptive understanding of the social forces shaping modern America, and his creative handling of the issues of institutional organization and control. Emerson's commitment to a social philosophy of radical individualism gave him no categories with which to grapple with the problems of a developing industrial society dominated by large bureaucracies; he might readily criticize, but he could not show how to control. Emerson's extreme spiritualization of religion left him with no doctrine of the church; small wonder that the so-called "free churches" he inspired quickly petered out and left no trace behind. It was Bellows who knew how to organize the United States Sanitary Commission during the Civil War, and the National Conference of Unitarian Churches after it. It was Bellows who realized that the organization of military and economic power by the North was transforming American society, and who began to ask what kind of religious and philanthropic institutions could operate effectively in this new environment. Emerson, the individualist, lived in a still-rural village; his is the eloquent voice of an age that survives today in nostalgic memory. Bellows, the institutional innovator, lived in a commercial metropolis; the world he attempted to understand and reform is recognizably the world we are still living in. No doubt when we look at ourselves in the mirror of history we should see Emerson; but there is something wrong if we do not also see Bellows.

Admittedly, it is not fashionable these days to say a good word for established institutions. To propose the canonization of an establishment man like Bellows may seem a hopelessly quixotic venture. Establishments are having a hard time of it at the moment. The Fifth French Republic is faced with an essentially revolutionary situation; the Soviet Union dares not intervene to prevent liberalization of the power structure in Czechoslovakia; Columbia University seethes with unresolved tensions; the mood in Resurrection City is one of frustration, and Washington does not know what may result; and Mayor Daley is not likely to have a restful summer. The legitimate complaints of alienated groups in this country command the sympathy of many of us: the young men who feel that it is only by resisting the draft that a genuine protest against the war is possible; the blacks who declare that tokenism is the most that the establishment is going to grant, and tokenism is not enough.

Yet we delude ourselves if we suppose that Unitarians and Universalists are not really part of the Establishment. We had a survey, not long ago, sponsored by the Goals Committee, which indicated that our membership is overwhelmingly concentrated in those socioeconomic classes from which decision-makers for American society are drawn. There may not be many Unitarian and Universalist decision-makers in the Pentagon; but there are plenty of them on college campuses, and we still like to boast of the high proportion of them in the United States Senate. The Establishment includes many different kinds of institutions; the Unitarian Universalist Association and the Meadville Theological School are among them.

Our choice is not between either being a part of the Establishment or rejecting it; our choice is to decide what kind of established institutions we are going to sustain. There are different kinds of establishments. One of them is the Bourbon Establishment, which never learns, and which is astonished when someone suggests that its privileges are not necessarily the reward of virtue. There is the authoritarian kind of establishment, which relies ultimately on the ruthless use of the instruments of coercive power. But there is also the kind of establishment without which neither democratic society nor liberal religion can long survive—an establishment which respects the continuity of institutional development, which is open to the future without repudiating the past, which is sensitive to the claims of disadvantaged groups without abdicating its own responsibilities, which seeks a proper distribution of power rather than a monopoly of it, which is not fearful of the corrupt use of power that it is too timid to use it wisely. This is the kind of establishment that Bellows tried to create; it is still the kind of establishment we need.

What the historian can do for us today is to remind us that this kind of establishment is not alien to our tradition, but actually very much a part of what we have been and are. We have been less discriminating than we ought to have been in our use of symbols drawn from the past, with the result that we tend to overemphasize the strain of radical individualism in our tradition. That part of our tradition all too often encourages us to abdicate responsibility for the nurture of our common institutional life; it is a measure of our failure to free ourselves from the irrelevancies of a dead past. It is through a tradition of responsible institutionalism that we shall discover how to meet the challenge of an uncertain future.

10

The Role of the Clergy
in the Shaping of Public Policy

——————◆——————

Address to the Massachusetts Convention of Ministers,
May 4, 1970. Earth Day was April 22;
the invasion of Cambodia was April 30;
the deaths at Kent State were on May 4, 1970.

The title of this address was selected some months ago, and it is
less precise than it ought to be. There is always a hazard in
committing oneself too far in advance to a particular formulation
of a topic; the right title is more likely to emerge in the process of
working through the material and ordering it for final presentation, not three months ahead of time. And so my first duty is to
clarify the intended scope of this discussion.

I propose then, to examine the process of decision-making in
our political institutions, and ask how people in the churches,
laity and ministers both, can most effectively influence that
process in order to promote sound public policy. To state it more
pointedly: given churches of the kind served by the members of
this convention, and assuming a widespread concern shared by
them on some grave issue of policy, how can that concern be
focussed so that it will influence the decision-makers who occupy positions of public trust, and thereby help to shape public
policy?

My interest in this subject is much less theoretical or philosophical than the announced title might suggest. I will attempt
to be essentially practical and concerned with the techniques by
which influence is exerted and made effective. Let me underline
the fact that I shall be talking about how ministers and lay people

can exert their influence, and not how they can mobilize political pressure. The argument I wish to advance is that ministers and lay leaders of our churches have many more opportunities for exerting influence than they ever take advantage of; indeed that they are favorably situated to make the weight of their influence felt. But through ignorance usually, through stupidity sometimes, and through perverseness often, they are tempted to dissipate that influence by various kinds of quixotic and unproductive behavior.

The structure of this talk will be very simple. First, I will examine a specific instance of decision-making, by which the direction of national policy on a major issue was reversed. The case study will be the sequence of events in March, 1968, which ended with President Johnson's decision to end military escalation in Vietnam, and to withdraw as a candidate for re-election. Then, after generalizing from that analysis, we shall turn our attention to the question of how you and I might have exerted some influence on the process culminating in those decisions. Are there points in the sequence of events leading to decisions of that kind where the particular influence that you and I can exert is most likely to be felt? And how can it be made effective?

In marshalling the factual data for the initial case study, I shall rely largely on two sources. One of them is Townsend Hoopses's book, *The Limits of Intervention*, recently published. The subtitle is: "An inside account of how the Johnson policy of escalation in Vietnam was reversed." The other source is an analysis of the same sequence of events prepared by Hedrick Smith of the *New York Times*, with the assistance of other members of the staff of that paper, and also published in 1969. I am also familiar with what President Johnson said when interviewed on television by Walter Cronkite. But the problems posed by his version are of a different kind, and had best be left to other occasions and other commentators.

The end of February, 1968, is a good point at which to pick up the threads of the story. The Tet offensive had begun a month earlier; and while that spasm had pretty well run its course in a military sense, its psychological impact was still great. The optimistic official interpretation was that it had been an act of desperation on the part of the Vietcong, who now were coming out of the countryside where they were elusive targets, to fight in the cities where our military power could get at them more easily. But those skeptical of official optimism asked how it happened that cities that were supposed to be safe had been devastated.

The military situation called for a reappraisal. General Earl Wheeler, Chairman of the Joint Chiefs of Staff, made a quick trip to Saigon, conferred with General Westmoreland, and returned on February 28 to present a request for 206,000 additional troops by the end of the year, with more than half of the increase coming in the next two months. This would have raised our commitment in troops to more than 700,000.

There were those in Washington who wondered why, if the Tet offensive had really been a disaster for the enemy, we should suddenly be called upon to provide a forty percent increase in troop strength. But the initial reaction was that some substantial part of the requested increase, at least, would be granted. Just how much, and on what schedule, was regarded as a matter for decision, not whether there would be any escalation at all.

Next we must examine the structure of authority in Washington to find out by whom, and under what influences, the decisions were made.

First of all, the role of the President must be considered. Admittedly, the chief executive does not personally make all the decisions made in his name. But the Vietnam War had been Johnson's central concern for many months, and the policy we were pursuing was one in which he had invested much of his ego. Any significant change in the direction of our policy, so long as Johnson was President, would require an altercation of his views; it was not going to be made by subordinates while his attention was elsewhere. Since Johnson had no doubts that the policy of this government was not only morally right, but prudentially sound and workable, most doves despaired of a shift of policy. There seemed to be no way to influence a stubborn and proud President who was convinced that history would prove him to have been right, and his clamorous critics wrong. Johnson had been a politician all his life, and as Senate leader had distinguished himself as a man who knew which policies could eventually command a consensus and which ones were not worth going down to defeat over. But as President, and especially on the issue of Vietnam, he gave every appearance of being unyielding.

For those who disapproved of our policy, the hopelessness of the situation seemed the more obvious as soon as one looked at Johnson's closest advisers. They included men like Dean Rusk, Walt Rostow, General Maxwell Taylor, Abe Fortas, and the newly appointed Secretary of Defense, Clark Clifford. All of them were understood to be hawks. Rusk tended to see aggression in Southeast Asia in the 1960s as the equivalent of Nazi aggression in the 1930s. His mind seemed imprisoned in a stereotyped analysis of the situation which pointed to an inevitable conclusion. General Taylor's involvement in the Vietnam situation dated from 1961, when Rostow and he had prepared the report that shifted our policy from one of giving advice to the South Vietnamese government to one of direct partnership with the Vietnamese. His conception of the problem was essentially a military one, and he was convinced throughout that a military solution was possible.

Walt Rostow had gone to Washington at the beginning of the Kennedy administration, only to be shunted off into a quiet corner of the State Department. But after McGeorge Bundy's departure in 1966, Rostow transferred to the White House as foreign policy coordinator and adviser to the President. Johnson found both the man and his views congenial, and his influence increased steadily. Townsend Hoopes describes Rostow's relationship to the President thus:

> By this time Rostow had become the channel through which President Johnson received almost all written communications on foreign affairs; he had, moreover, a large hand in determining who, outside the closed circle of advisers, the President would see or not see. He possessed great weight on Vietnam policy because he was both physically close and intellectually reassuring to the President. Rostow briefed him each morning, saw

him several times a day, and selected the papers for his night reading. Astride the main channel, he could develop for the President all of the options, or some; could pass along all the views expressed by responsible department heads and their staffs, or some; could send them forward without comment, or with his own recommendations. It was a position of great temptation for a dedicated partisan whose mind automatically filtered out evidence that did not support his own established beliefs.

Rusk, Taylor, and Rostow had been close to the President over a period of many months. Clark Clifford, on the other hand, was assuming his duties as Secretary of Defense as of March 1, 1968, and represented a new factor in the equation. In light of his record, there was no reason to suppose that he would do anything other than reinforce the hawkish atmosphere of Johnson's inner circle. Secretary McNamara had become increasingly uneasy about our policy and a less than reliable spokesperson for it; this tendency would seem to have been a factor in his departure for the World Bank. But Clifford, everyone assumed, would restore the harmony of the inner circle. He had the reputation of being a hawk; and as he assumed office, he had no though of an alteration in the basic direction of policy.

In addition to this circle of inner advisers, the President also relied on a larger but less intimate body called the Senior Advisory Group on Vietnam. It included men not currently holding governmental positions, but who had had wide experience in foreign affairs. Among them were Dean Acheson, McGeorge Bundy, Douglas Dillon, General Omar Bradley, and others. As recently as October, 1967, this group had reviewed and reaffirmed our policy in Southeast Asia.

One other element in the power structure needs to be identified. Within the Pentagon itself, as Clifford soon discovered, there was a nest of doves, which included some of his immediate subordinates. Among them were Paul Nitze, Deputy Secretary of Defense; Paul Warneke, Assistant Secretary for International Security Affairs; and Townsend Hoopes, Under Secretary of the

Air Force. Some of these men had had doubts about our policy ever since 1965. These doubts became insistent in 1967; the Tet offensive, Mr. Hoopes tells us, had been a sort of moment of truth when real opinions came out into the open. But these assistant secretaries and undersecretaries despaired of having any influence on policy, despite the responsible positions they filled, so inaccessible seemed the President's circle of advisers. Some had wondered whether they should resign in protest; or had debated with themselves under what circumstances they would feel obliged to resign.

Clifford arrived on the scene just as the request for 206,000 additional troops precipitated a general review of policy. An *ad hoc* task force was set up by the President, chaired by Clifford, whose assignment apparently was expected to be to determine how best to give General Westmoreland what he needed. But Clifford had not insulated himself from diverse opinions, and was already aware of the unrest felt by an increasing number of his subordinates. He enlarged the discussion to include the basic question whether our policy itself was a viable one. For the first time, alternative views were being seriously considered close to the centers of power.

After a week of discussion, a preliminary and tentative memorandum was drawn up, which called for 20,000 additional troops at once but deferment of a decision on the balance of the request, together with a stepping-up of the bombing. When Clifford presented these recommendations to the President on March 8, he stressed their tentative character, and intimated that he himself was somewhat uneasy about them. A certain coolness between the President and his new Secretary of Defense seems to have been the consequence.

Mid-March brought the New Hampshire primary, and Robert Kennedy's decision to seek the Democratic nomination. Such developments were calculated to make Johnson more adamant, not less. "Let's get one thing clear," he declared. "I am not going to stop the bombing. I have heard every argument on the subject, and I am not interested in further discussion. I have made up my mind. I'm not going to stop it."

Yet it was at just about this time that Clifford had finally sorted out the policy options in his own mind, and found himself agreeing more and more with the view that the Administration's policy could not be defended. The President might wall himself off from the dovish opinions of assistant secretaries and under-secretaries; but Clifford could not. These men had access to him, as they had not to the President; and the considerations they presented to him were persuasive. Yet Clifford's demurrers at first made no impression on the President either. Instead Johnson made bellicose speeches on March 18 and 19.

The next crucial event was a meeting of the Senior Advisory Group on Vietnam, on March 25 and 26. Six months earlier, the Group had reaffirmed our policy. Now, to Johnson's shock, it appeared that the overwhelming majority had turned towards de-escalation, disengagement, and an end of the bombing. The President's staff had been working on a major policy speech for him, and all the preliminary drafts had been written on the assumption that further escalation was coming. But Clifford told the President bluntly that the speech he was planning to deliver three days later would be a disaster; that what he needed was not a war speech, but a peace speech. Three days later, on March 31, Johnson delivered the peace speech, and announced he would not be a candidate in November.

These events are likely to be discussed for years to come, as a case study in top-level decision-making. It is not often that we learn with so little delay as much as this about the inner process by which a major decision was made. Certain crucial aspects of the process need to be emphasized.

(1) Neither public opinion, nor congressional criticism, nor student protests, nor the opposition of the Kennedys had any discernible influence on Johnson's decision. So far as he was concerned, this seems to have been a case where he felt it his duty to adhere to a policy he believed to be the right one, and leave it to posterity to vindicate him. With others, under other circum-stances, such firmness in the right as God gives them to see the right has been described as an act of the highest courage.

(2) What did change Johnson's mind and persuade him to take a new course of action was the direct personal influence of

people like Clifford on whom he had long relied, and whose loyalty he had always taken for granted. Though public opinion at large might not budge him, it was devastating when the Cliffords, and the Achesons, and the Goldbergs, and the McGeorge Bundys, some of them fellow-architects of the policy he was following, now began to tell him he was on the wrong track. Against his enemies, his critics, and the anonymous voice of the public he had ample defenses. He had none to shield him from his friends.

(3) The change of policy began, not with the President, or even with immediate subordinates, such as the Secretary of Defense. The change began at a third level in the decision-making hierarchy—with the Paul Nitzes, the Townsend Hoopeses, and the Paul Warnekes. These men had been frustrated throughout 1967 because all channels of communication upward to the President seemed blocked. They were nevertheless ready when simultaneously Clifford's appointment and the Tet offensive gave them hope that their voices might be listened to. Hoopes and Clifford were already on first-name terms; and on February 13, after Clifford had been confirmed by the Senate, but before he had assumed office, Hoopes sent him a long personal letter arguing that bombing in North Vietnam had no effect on the number of American casualties in South Vietnam. In mid-March, he forwarded to Clifford an inclusive memorandum, marshalling the arguments that military victory in Vietnam was not feasible. Others in the Defense Department, whom Clifford likewise knew personally, were making comparable presentations to him. Clifford's willingness to take a fresh look at the entire range of policy options was crucial. But so too were the views of his dovish subordinates, some of whom he had known personally for a long time. Without them, there is every reason to suppose, Clifford's own doubts and questionings would have been stifled, and Johnson would have gone forward with his original version of the speech of March 31. Then surely we would have been neck-deep, and not just waist-deep, in the Big Muddy.

So much for our case study, and the conclusions we can draw as to how decisions were reached in that particular instance.

Now we must attempt some larger generalizations about how our concerns may be translated into public policy and implemented by political decisions. Here we may begin by distinguishing three ways by which individuals and groups may work for political ends.

(1) The first of these is through an appeal to public opinion. Not much is going to happen—except of a routine bureaucratic kind—unless some segment of the public becomes vocal about it. The appeal to public opinion has two related objectives. On the one hand it seeks to educate and inform people so that they will realize what is at stake, and in many instances they will discover that they have a lot at stake. An Earth Day, for example, is not immediately translated into legislation; it serves rather to heighten the sensitivity of large numbers of people to the problems of pollution, population, and the environment. But on the other hand, the appeal to public opinion may also be aimed at persuading legislators and public officials that a particular concern is widely shared in the community, and therefore one to which they must give attention. Mass meetings or demonstrations, if they are to be useful instruments, must have this simple and uncomplicated objective. The point that the demonstration must seek to make is that there is widespread popular support for a given policy. It must enlarge its appeal by emphasizing a simple, easily stated policy option, not a detailed policy proposal.

Mass demonstrations are not the only way of appealing to public opinion. It is hard to avoid some stress on them at the moment, since they have been a characteristic part of our recent experience. But every time an individual writes a letter to the editor, or joins with others in a full-page ad in the *New York Times*, or writes an article for a current journal of opinion, an attempt is made to create a favorable climate within which a particular policy may be adopted or implemented. One does not have to take to the streets to engage in relevant action.

(2) In addition to the appeal to public opinion, there may be efforts to organize political power and exert political pressure. Public support for a given policy has to be made effective through some form of political process. Sooner or later this

involves local organization, the support of some candidates and the defeat of others, and reminders to legislators that elections come around on schedule and that it may make a difference to them if organized groups of citizens are working for them rather than for the opposition. The organization of political power, whether through pressure groups or through party machinery, is laborious and time-consuming. It obviously will not appeal to the seekers of instant Utopia.

(3) Finally, there is the use of influence. This aspect of the political process seems to be the one least well understood by the ordinary citizen-reformer. Yet it must be recalled that it was not public opinion, nor was it organized political pressure, that reversed the policy of escalation and made a President announce his retirement. It was influence, direct personal influence exerted within the highest circles of the Administration. We should not allow ourselves to be deluded on this point; we should not succumb to the popular myth-making that would have us believe that Johnson responded to popular agitation. McCarthy's children's crusade in New Hampshire was important, not because it changed Johnson's mind, but because it increased the credibility of Clifford's arguments. The crux of the matter was personal influence: the influence on the President of Clark Clifford and members of the Senior Advisory Group; the influence on Clifford of Warneke, and Hoopes, and others two steps removed from the White House.

Why is it that we pay so little attention to the role of personal influence in the decision-making process, and therefore develop no strategy for its use? I suppose it is because it seems to be so idiosyncratic and dependent on the particular individuals who happen to be exercising certain functions at a given time. Often such lines of influence are informal and unstructured, bypassing the routine channels of command and communication. Hence they have an air of illegitimacy about them, as somehow more appropriate for a government of royal favorites than one of laws. They have an air of illegality to them, as though they simply involved special favors in return for campaign contributions, or for gifts that can hardly be distinguished from bribes. They seem unreliable, since patterns of influence are constantly shifting, like watercourses in the braided delta of a river. They have an air of secrecy about them, since the outsider finds it hard to tell who really counts in a bureaucratic structure, and assumes something is wrong if it does not operate according to the plan of organization. Who from the outside can perceive the Pentagon, with its 5,000 inhabitants, as held together by a network of interpersonal relationships?

We have all had experiences of our own that should remind us of the role personal influence plays throughout all bureaucratic structures. One small and homely example comes to my mind. After the Second World War it was proposed in the City of Cambridge to build a war memorial swimming pool adjacent to the High and Latin School, which would be open both to the school children and to the public at large. There was a privately-owned apartment building on the proposed site, an old-fashioned structure that had long been a favorite lodging for graduate students. The owners were not unwilling to sell, but their price was higher than the city thought it proper to pay. The negotiations seemed to be dragging on with no discernible progress, and some began to wonder whether it might be necessary to take possession by eminent domain. Then, unexpectedly, the announcement was made that an acceptable settlement had been reached.

What had happened? The most obvious thing was that a new city solicitor had been appointed. That fact indeed had a bearing on the situation. But there was more to it than might be appreciated by the casual observer. The new city solicitor was, or had recently been, a member of the Standing Committee of the First Parish in Cambridge; the lawyer acting for the owners was also a member of that Committee. Their personal friendship made a quick settlement possible, not because a deal resulted, but because there was an atmosphere of confidence, which enabled counsel to reach an agreement satisfactory to both parties.

Such experiences remind us that within those bureaucratic structures that we call collectively "the Establishment," decisions are dependent on the quality of interpersonal contacts, and the character of the network of relationships that they form.

Personal influence is not an external element illegitimately smuggled into the organizational structure, even though it may be illegitimately used. Rather the organizational structure is a complex of channels that facilitate the flow of such influence. When the networks of interpersonal relationships work well, the organization looks good, no matter how illogical its formal structure may be. When those networks work badly, the most beautiful organizational chart ever constructed won't save you.

So we come at last to the question of whether or how it is possible for us—for you and me, who hold no official posts in Washington—to influence political decisions. Are we restricted to activities that involve the shaping of public opinion, or organization to exert political pressure? Is this what "working within the system" means for us? Or are there channels of influence available, if we have wit to discover them and sense to use them intelligently, that extend from the points of crucial decision-making out into the community at large?

If the Massachusetts Convention of Ministers were made up of part-time Pentecostal ministers from store-front churches, ministering to Spanish-speaking Puerto Ricans in the South End of Boston, the answer might be *No*. There *are* segments of society cut off from access to the key decision-makers, even from decision-making in Boston City Hall, let alone in the State Department in Washington. For such people, personal influence counts for nothing; and if their needs are to be met by political processes, their leaders have to work out a dual strategy of political pressure and the appeal to public opinion. There *are* alienated and disadvantaged groups in society, and they are restricted accordingly in the ways by which they can press their claims and speak to the consciences of the more fortunate.

But the ministers of this Convention are part of the Establishment, so called, whether they like it or not. It is irresponsible and romantic rhetoric when they talk, some of them, as though they belonged to the alienated and forgotten fragments of society. That may be a way to rid oneself of feelings of guilt; but ritual self-purgings of that sort have not in the past been known to have much impact on the Pentagon or the White House. The issues that concern us, whether in Vietnam or in the ghetto, are too important for us to do anything except deal with them with the most effective instruments available to us.

As members of the Establishment, gentlemen of the Convention, you possess personal influence and access to the channels by which it can be exerted. You have an enormous advantage in this respect over members of various other groups in American society; for personal influence can be an instrument of considerable precision and effectiveness. Weigh, if you will, the comparative advantages of your signature along with 999 others in small type in an advertisement in the Boston *Globe*, or on a petition containing 5,000 names of obscure citizens, and that same signature at the bottom of a personal letter to an official in Washington who helps to shape the atmosphere within which great decisions are made, and who at the same time has some sense of identification with you to command attention to what you say. Maybe it is important for your name to appear in the Boston *Globe*; I do not presume to pass judgment on that. Maybe signing a petition or two does some real good; though I suspect it does more to quiet your conscience than to arouse the conscience of the official to which it is addressed. But I would argue that you are not a good steward of your talents unless you take advantage of what is peculiarly yours—the opportunity to exert personal influence.

Some of you may be inwardly protesting that you are not personal friends of the President, or of his Secretary of Defense; and so these admonitions do not apply to you. So let's try a practical experiment together. I suspect that there are few people, if any, in the congregation today who are personal friends of President Nixon. His religious tastes would seem to run in other directions. But there may be a few among you who know personally some individual who in turn knows the President. On the other hand, I suspect that most of the people here today know someone who knows someone else who knows President Nixon. Indeed, if you start to think over in your own mind the number of different channels of interpersonal relationships that could take you to the President with only two intermediate steps, I venture to say that many of you would find half a dozen of them. Most of you know someone who knows Governor Volpe. Some of you may know someone who knows Pat Moynihan. Some of you may know someone who knows Elliot Richardson, and so on. I suggest that each one of us can trace out a few of these lines of interpersonal relationships connecting him with the White House. How many of you can reach President Nixon with only *one* intermediate step? How many of you can do it with no more than *two* intermediate steps?

My point here is not to persuade you that you now have a way to get to the ear of the President, so that your arguments will be immediately accepted, and your policies promptly implemented. It is merely to try to give you a feel for the Establishment as a complicated network of interpersonal relationships of which you are a part; in fact, a not so very remote part.

Our earlier analysis indicated that President Johnson's decision to halt escalation began not with him but with assistant secretaries and undersecretaries a couple of levels below him in the decision-making structure. So we need not be concerned if we see no immediate prospect of getting President Nixon's ear. He's not the immediate target. The more vulnerable objective is made up of the functionaries lower down, who do the staff work on which the top level decision-makers depend. These officials get fewer letters and are more likely to read them, especially if the personal relationship can be established.

This is not to say that government personnel at the working level can force policy on those above them. But top level policy cannot be maintained indefinitely against the drag that can develop in the bureaucratic structure. At this very juncture it is clear that President Nixon has uncertain control over the bureaucracy, large segments of which are as distrustful of his Cambodian venture as any doves in the Senate, or in this room. One newspaper columnist recently wrote: "Throughout the government, at the working level below that of the policy makers, there is understood to have been strong opposition to widening the war in Cambodia and distress at the way things were developing." The columnist continues: "These people are said to have done the planning and research jobs asked of them. But many made no attempt to hide their heaviness of heart and their belief that the Cambodian operations would become an even bigger quagmire for America, not the shortcut to ending the war, which Mitchell and the military chiefs believed." Sentiment of this kind within the Establishment in Washington is a factor of incalculable consequences; and it represents the first step toward the time when President Nixon will press the buzzer and no one will respond. The academic and ecclesiastical establishments outside Washington have much contact with this level of the official Federal Establishment; the opportunity to exert influence through them needs to be exploited.

Even where no direct personal relationships exist, personal influence can still be exerted to a significant degree, provided some basis of identification can be established. Were a member of my college class, for example, to accept a position of responsibility in Washington, I imagine I could succeed in writing to him a letter that would intimate that people like himself whose favorable opinion is important to him are going to be watching his career; and are—shall we say—eager to help him make wise decisions. If this classmate of mine also happened to be from Massachusetts, and even happened to be of all things a Unitarian, the basis for identification and response would be even more firm and obvious.

The objective here is to get your views on a matter of public policy to the attention of those who participate in the shaping of that policy. A letter that is actually read by an Undersecretary or Bureau Chief is more important than one that is in the middle of a pile and weighed in quantity at the White House. My own experience is that this line of approach does work; and while my influence on the President is still not as great as that of Secretary Mitchell, there may be some less prominent official whose resolution has been strengthened against the war, and whose influence will be felt when a crisis comes—as it will come—when the situation breaks open, as it did once before in 1968.

I would not be understood. I am not saying that to exert personal pressure makes it any less important these days to organize politically for the support of the right candidates, or that the familiar ways of seeking to influence public opinion may be abandoned. I do think that if you expect to exert influence, you had better not go trashing; there are certain kinds of appeal to public opinion that are incompatible with effective personal influence. But the link must be made between public opinion, political organization, and the ultimate goal of decision-making; personal influence is a considerable part of what brings them together. There is work to be done. We all have something to contribute; let us be about the task.

11

Individualism in Historical Perspective

◆

Address at the conference of
Unitarian Universalist Advance,
Cambridge, Massachusetts, May, 1979

Although I am by profession an historian, what I have in mind here is not so much historical analysis as cultural commentary; I think it only fair to make that clear at the outset. I will, however, look at certain historical figures, and it is only proper that they be represented accurately, and their views not deliberately and egregiously distorted.

But I am proposing to take them as representative of certain major strands in our culture. That will involve judgments on my part that these individuals may properly be regarded as representative, and that the cultural tendencies they will symbolize are identifiable and significant. Historical analysis and historical judgment may easily become subservient to other uses, and criticism of this presentation will have to differentiate between questions of demonstrable error, and questions of the acceptability of the judgments involved in the selection of historical examples.

But there is more to it than that. For I intend to try to identify certain conditions under which the cultural tendencies represented by the chosen figures have emerged and flourished. This will involve a correlation between social situations and ideology of a kind that does not lend itself to exact demonstration and proof. I do not think it improper for historians to engage in this kind of juggling of such high-level abstractions as "individual-ism." But what may persuade me that a particular correlation is plausible may involve obscure and half-acknowledged parts of my own past experience, which conditions the perspective from which I view the limited hard-core objective data on which the correlation is formally made to rest.

But if a correlation may be asserted between certain social situations in the past and a particular ideology, the implication is that a change in the social environment will sooner or later result in alterations in the ideology. If we project recent social trends into the future and begin to predict what is likely to happen to familiar patterns of thought as a consequence, we need to keep in mind that prediction is an uncertain science at best, and historians cannot claim to be better at it than anyone else.

And if, finally, we make some specific application to the future of liberal religion in the kind of world that we are project-ing, we enter a realm of discussion in which each one may express an opinion, but only the event will demonstrate who has been right and who has been wrong.

All this is a reminder that the purpose of this presentation is not primarily to convey information, though it may include some; nor does it assume that agreement among us will result. Disagreement is to be expected and welcomed. If factual errors emerge, they may be noted and corrected; but the argument floats free of any *particular* set of facts, though not of factual basis altogether. If discussion promotes a common understanding, well and good; but the exercise can be worthwhile even if no agreement results. And if the conclusions commend themselves to no one else, I shall not worry. I can always be content as a work-a-day historian, busy with a detailed reconstruction of the controversy in the Second Church in Dorchester, or rearguing the legal issues in the Dedham case.

Let us now turn to the first of two historical figures, chosen as representative of a major cultural strand in American life: Thomas Jefferson, exponent of the Enlightenment in America, spokesman for the Age of Reason.

It is Jefferson's views on religion, particularly, that we must examine. What were they? Unitarians have been especially interested in the question, hoping to add another President to the beadroll of Unitarian saints and worthies that has often been the stock in trade of writers of promotional pamphlets published by the UUA. One Thomas Jefferson would surely be worth half-a-dozen Millard Fillmores. After all, did not Jefferson write to Benjamin Waterhouse: "I trust that there is not a *young man* now living in the United States who will not die a Unitarian"? Or again: "The population of my neighborhood is too slender, and is too much divided into other sects to maintain any one preacher well. I must therefore be contented to be a Unitarian by myself "[1]

Scholars interested in Jefferson's religion have generally sought to define it by comparison or contrast with that of others whose doctrinal positions are clearer and better understood. One scholar, half a century ago, reached the conclusion that Jefferson was not a Unitarian because his Christology was markedly different from that of Channing, who might properly be taken as a standard. But Henry Wilder Foote, twenty years later, rightly pointed out that Jefferson knew and admired Joseph Priestley, and often went to hear him preach in the 1790s. Priestley's Christology was different from that of Channing; his Unitarianism was of the English and not the New English sort. But Unitarianism it was, none the less. "I am not aware of the peculiar resistance to Unitarianism, which you ascribe to Pennsylvania," Jefferson wrote in 1822. "When I lived in Pennsylvania there was a respectable congregation of that sect, with a meetinghouse and regular service which I attended, and in which Doctor Priestley officiated to numerous audiences." On the strength of testimony such as this, Dr. Foote had no hesitation in claiming Jefferson.

Actually, the matter is not quite so simple. If we are to judge by the composite life of Jesus as compiled by Jefferson from the four gospels, Jefferson's view of Jesus differed from that of

---

[1] Henry Wilder Foote, *The Religion of Thomas Jefferson* (Boston, 1960), p. 76. [Original title: *Thomas Jefferson: Champion of Religious Freedom, Advocate of Christian Morals* (Boston, 1947).]

Priestley as well as from that of Channing. When Jefferson was done, all the miraculous or supernatural elements had been excised from the text, leaving the ethical teachings as the essential heart of the gospels. This leaves it a question as to whether, in any sense, Jefferson would have agreed with Priestley that Christianity is a divinely revealed religion, attested by the evidences of prophecy and miracles. Or to put it another way, it is still not clear whether Jefferson was a Deist—and so no more than a partly sympathetic fellow-traveler of Unitarians like Priestley—or whether he was a Supernatural Rationalist, and therefore clearly in accord with Priestley, and Channing, and all the other Unitarians until the Transcendentalists came along to change the categories altogether.[2]

Yet all this discussion of Jefferson's doctrinal position misses the point in one crucial respect. For perhaps the most important thing to be said about Jefferson's religious position is that we do not really know what the doctrinal content of it was. If ever there was a person who insisted that religion is a private matter, it was Jefferson. He did so, not simply because his views were unorthodox and so would have exposed him to political attack, of which there was enough anyway, but because he held to a view of religion that was individualistic in the extreme. "I inquire after no man's religious opinions," he wrote, "and trouble none with mine."

Jefferson's extreme privatization of religion amounts to an assertion as to the nature of religion. He thought of religion, essentially, as a set of opinions about God, our obligations to him as individuals, and the system of morals that results. This view of religion runs all the way through the Virginia Act for Establishing Religious Freedom (1786) of which Jefferson was the author. The Act was concerned with protecting the individual's right to adhere to whatever set of religious opinions commended themselves to him. The text of the Act condemns those who set

---

[2] For a definition of Supernatural Rationalism and a discussion of its dissemination, see Conrad Wright, *The Liberal Christians* (Boston, 1970), pp.1-21. An excellent discussion of Jefferson's religious views is: Eugene R. Sheridan, "Introduction" to *Jefferson's Extracts from the Gospels*, ed. Dickenson W. Adams (Princeton, N.J., 1983).

up "their own opinions and modes of thinking as the only true and infallible"; it argues that one should not be taxed "for the propagation of opinions which he disbelieves"; it rejects the notion that a magistrate should "intrude his powers into the field of opinion"; it declares that no one should suffer "on account of his religious opinions or belief." The word "opinion" is used no less than nine times in Jefferson's text.

Freedom of thought and expression is a cherished value, and Jefferson's writings make the point emphatically that religious truth, like other kinds of truth, has nothing to fear from an open clash with error, and needs no State establishment to sustain it. Probably we would agree that that is a valuable contribution to the creation of a sound tradition on matters of Church and State. But other consequences of his extraordinarily limited definition of religion are not so helpful. How limited and limiting that definition is becomes apparent when one asks what the function of churches and other ecclesiastical institutions might be. Is the Church for Jefferson anything more than a group of persons assembled more or less fortuitously to hear promulgated a particular set of religious opinions? But if such religious opinions can be communicated in other ways, is the Church a necessary institution? Thomas Jefferson could sit quietly in his library and read Priestley's *History of the Corruptions of Christianity*. Why would that not be just as good as listening to Priestley preach on the same subject? Why would not it be better? For Jefferson the Church was an institution that presumably did not harm, so long as it did not attempt to force its views on others; and people should be free to gather for common religious instruction if they chose. But there was nothing in Jefferson's understanding of religion that required people to form religious communities or explained why they persistently seek religious fellowship—nothing derived from laws of human nature, let alone any commandment from God.

Jefferson's understanding of the nature of religion—this definition of religion as first and foremost a set of doctrines or opinions to be rationally assessed, and accepted or rejected by an individual act of judgment—was not peculiar to him. The rational half of the eighteenth century, as distinguished from the evangelical, pietistic, and revivalistic half, took it for granted that there are basic truths of religion to be established by the power of Reason, which is a faculty common to all human beings (except of course newborn babies and idiots). John Locke's *Essay Concerning Human Understanding* (1691) had laid the philosophical foundations for the kind of religion that Jefferson espoused. Locke's definition of Man assumes the individual self as the unit, self-sufficient in the sense of possessing the faculty of Reason, for whom society is constructed by the separate action of individuals, and not an expression of something inherent in human nature itself. In Locke's political theory, individuals give up their complete freedom and autonomy in the State of Nature for prudential reasons only. There is something to be gained thereby, but there is always the sense of regret at the unfortunate necessity that requires corporate action; the implication is that the individual is diminished in consequence. So with Jefferson and the church: religion remains a private possession because there is nothing in his understanding of it that suggests that religious fellowship has any value, or that there is anything in human nature that needs religious community.

We turn now from Jefferson, representing eighteenth-century rational religion, to Ralph Waldo Emerson, who stands for nineteenth-century romanticism, and for Transcendentalism in particular.

The first thing that must always be said when interpreting Emerson's religious position, is that he consciously and deliberately rejected the tradition for which Locke was one of the formulators and of which Jefferson was an exponent. The rationalistic Christian apologetics to which it gave rise seemed to Emerson to be corpse-cold. Religion, Emerson insisted, is not simply a set of opinions validated by discursive reasoning by argumentation. It is first of all an experience of sublimity and wonder that touches the inmost being. In his book *Nature* Emerson says "Crossing a bare common, in snow puddles, at twilight, under a clouded sky, without having in my thoughts any occurrence of special good fortune, I have enjoyed a perfect exhilaration. I am glad to the brink of fear." Such moments

Emerson referred to as "landmarks of the soul" and to them he ascribed more of the reality than to all the prosaic existence that lies between. "What is all this," he asked, "but the one Fact, the one and only good news, matter of congratulation mutually between all rational agents throughout the Universe. We have found at last that there *is* something, and instantly all that we called Heaven and Earth have become a pale appearance. Then they glow again, new created by *it*. "

There is a profound difference in epistemology between the eighteenth-century rationalists and the nineteenth-century romantics. The rationalists proved the existence of God by intellectual demonstration from the Creation that we experience through the senses:

> The spacious firmament on high
> And all the blue ethereal sky
> And spangled heavens, a shining frame
> Their great Original proclaim.

That quotation is from Joseph Addison. But Wordsworth responded:

> And I have felt
> A presence that disturbs me with the joy
> Of elevated thoughts; a sense sublime
> Of something far more deeply interfused,
> Whose dwelling is the light of setting suns,
> And the round ocean and the living air,
> And the blue sky, and in the mind of man:
> A motion and a spirit, that impels
> All thinking things, all objects of all thought,
> And rolls through all things.

But just because Emerson rejects much that Jefferson stands for, that does not mean that he is opposite to him in all respects. For if Jefferson's view of religion is individualistic and privatized, so too is Emerson's. And if Jefferson's principles can yield no rationale for religious fellowship in general or the Church in particular, neither can Emerson's. The inward religious experience that Emerson prizes is even less communicable than the individual religious opinions that Jefferson was alert to protect. Though Emerson may assert a universality in such experience, so that the individual merges in the tides of being that flow through all things, such universality pulls him away from his fellow human beings; it does not draw him to them.

> Standing on the bare ground,—my head bathed by the blithe air, and uplifted into infinite space,—all mean egotism vanishes. I become a transparent eyeball; I am nothing; I see all; the currents of Universal Being circulate through me; I am part or parcel of God. The name of the nearest friend sounds then foreign and accidental: to be brothers, to be acquaintances, master or servant, is then a trifle and a disturbance.

Of course there was a lot of prosaic existence to be endured *between* Emerson's moments of ecstasy, his landmarks of the soul. It would not have been illogical if he had developed a doctrine of the Church that would acknowledge the significance of fellowship and community for the common level of experience, allowing for supreme moments of insight that transcended it. Yet Emerson never explored such possibilities. "Men descend to meet," he writes; for the individual that means a loss of integrity and consequently of power.

Not all Transcendentalists drew the conclusion that Emerson did, that the Church is to be contrasted with the Soul, rather than that the Soul finds some measure of its fulfillment in religious association. Not all would have agreed that the life of the soul lived in its fullness makes the church unnecessary. But it is Emerson whom we have canonized; and where will one find in all of his writings even the most rudimentary elements of a doctrine of the Church?

Emerson did publish a volume of essays entitled *Society and Solitude,* and one might hope to find there, if not a discussion of the Church, at least some indication of the kind of association among human beings that would commend itself to him. There is no essay there on the Church; but there is one on Clubs. In it there is an acknowledgment that there is something to be said for the mutual stimulus that thinkers discover when brought together. Of all the cordials known to us, Emerson writes, "the best, safest, and most exhilarating, with the least harm, is society; and every healthy and efficient mind passes a large part of life in the company most easy to him."

One may want to question the "most easy to him" aspect of it; but this begins to look like a doctrine of society applicable to the Church, until a bit farther on we find a sentence beginning: "If men are less together than they are alone . . . " And here we are back to a realization that for Emerson the individual is paramount; the infinity of the individual soul when fully realized makes social relationships trivial; society has nothing to offer in its own right, but only as a stimulus to the individual to recapture that self-sufficiency that will make society irrelevant.

Only a special kind of social relationship appeals to Emerson—one that provides the occasion for stimulating conversation. Ideal society finds exemplification, therefore, in the Transcendental Club early in Emerson's career, and the Saturday Club, meeting at dinner at the Parker House later on. If we may extrapolate a concept of religious association from that, a church would be a talking club of individualists mutually stimulating each other to be individualists, or at least to talk like individualists.

There have been and are religious groups of that kind, and there have been and are people who think that such groups represent the exalted ideal towards which we should be striving in our corporate religious life. But the problems with that model loom ominously large. It implies the omission of worship as a corporate act, necessarily involving subordination of individual preferences. It provides no adequate basis for continuing labor towards the transformation of the social order, which requires organization, some measure of discipline, and a lot of compromise. And at the most elementary level, it gives no assurance of institutional survival.

"The individual is the world," wrote Emerson; and when he sought to describe his own times, he found the clue to its understanding in that perception.

> It is the age of severance, of dissociation, of freedom, of analysis, of detachment. Every man for himself . . . The social sentiments are weak; the sentiment of patriotism is weak; veneration is low; the natural affections feebler than they were . . . There is an universal resistance to ties and ligaments once supposed essential to civil society . . . The age tends to solitude. The association of the time is accidental and momentary and hypocritical, the detachment intrinsic and progressive.

In Jefferson and Emerson, the tendency towards the privatization of religion, and consequently the atrophy of its corporate dimension, was carried further than it was by other religious liberals. Yet Emerson's atomic individualism is merely a more extreme version of tendencies widely apparent. Even religious liberals, like Henry W. Bellows, who boldly challenged this drift toward individualism, acknowledged its dominating power. Individualism, Bellows argued, is the inevitable tendency of the Protestant Reformation. Of course, he said, tendencies are not always ultimated; they encounter resistance. But "the sufficiency of the Scriptures turns out to be the self-sufficiency of man, and the right of private judgment an absolute independence of Bible or Church."

> No creed but the Scriptures, practically abolishes all Scriptures but those on the human heart; nothing between a man's conscience and his God, vacates the Church; and with the Church, the Holy Ghost, whose function is usurped by private reason; the Church lapses into what are called Religious Institutions; these into Congregationalism, and Congregationalism into Individualism— and the logical end is the abandonment of the Church as an independent institution . . . and the extinction of worship as a separate interest.[3]

---

[3] Henry W. Bellows, *The Suspense of Faith* (New York, 1859), p. 10.

Individualism, then, is not the only tendency operative in modern culture. Nor, indeed, has it been accepted as an unambiguously good thing among Unitarians and Universalists. But there is a continuous liberal tradition in politics and religion, going back to the seventeenth century, which seeks to free the individual from shackles of superstition, poverty, governmental control, and the pressures of mass opinion. Individualism in this tradition is seen as a liberating force, which will enable men and women to be more truly themselves and to find the experiences of life more fulfilling. At the same time, it is thought, it will release energies that will flow into a myriad of channels, artistic and cultural as well as purely material, so that a higher level of civilization is the result.

Now we must ask the question: why has individualism had this appeal, from Locke, to Jefferson, to Emerson, to John Stuart Mill, and on down to the present—at least in the West, and especially in America? Here we find ourselves involved in some of those broad and imprecise correlations that we must approach with caution. In order to keep the argument reasonably under control, I shall begin with a limited illustration of a shift from corporate identity to individualism. It is the shift from the communal society of the seventeenth-century New England Puritan to the more individualistic society of the eighteenth-century Yankee.

The social theory of the first settlers of Massachusetts Bay finds expression in John Winthrop's *Modell of Christian Charity*, the lay sermon he preached aboard the *Arbella* in 1630. The burden of the sermon was stated thus: "God Almightie in his most holy and wise providence hath soe disposed of the Condicion of mankinde, as in all times some must be rich some poore, some highe and eminent in power and dignitie; others meane and in subieccion." That in itself is enough to identify Winthrop as no liberal democrat. His was essentially a medieval concept of society, in which the parts are not equivalent and self-sufficient, but all, different in character and function, are necessary to the well-being of the whole, as the whole is necessary for the health of each. We might call this an organic view of society: the heart and the lungs cannot live on their own; but equally they are necessary for the health of the whole body.

It follows, therefore, that our survival as individuals involves a willingness to yield private preference to public necessities, "for it is a true rule that perticular estates cannott subsist in the ruine of the publique."

> ... wee must be knitt together in this worke as one man, wee must entertaine each other in brotherly Affeccion, wee must be willing to abridge our selues of our superfluities, for the supply of others necessities, wee must vphold a familiar Commerce together in all meekenes, gentlenes, patience and liberallity, wee must delight in eache other, make others Condicions our owne reioyce together, mourne together, labour and suffer together, allwayes haueing before our eyes our Commission and Community in the worke, our Community as members of the same body, soe shall we keepe the vnitie of the spirit in the bond of peace, the Lord will be our God and delight to dwell among vs, as his owne people and will commaund a blessing vpon vs in all our wayes . . .[4]

The institutions set up by the Massachusetts Bay Puritans were in accordance with this social theory. The congregational churches, brought into being by covenants, established mutual obligations as well as individual privileges for church members. The political order assumed the acceptance by all the inhabitants of a common unitive value system, and so those were excluded who, like Roger Williams, the Quakers, and the Antinomians, seemed to be a threat to the consensus on which the society rested.

Not least in importance as an expression of corporate solidarity was the land policy of the very first colonists. In a number of instances, towns in the Massachusetts Bay Colony were settled by groups of people who migrated together and were

---

[4] Perry Miller and Thomas H. Johnson, *The Puritans* (Boston and New York, 1938), pp. 195, 197, 198.

already gathered into church order. In any event, they built their meetinghouses and dwellings in a compact settlement, so that all might be under common watch and care. Sometimes, though not invariably, they perpetuated the common field system of land distribution. In any case, the agricultural land was within walking distance of the settlement—there were no isolated farmhouses.

One such town, *viz.*, Dedham, has been examined in detail by Professor Kenneth A. Lockridge, who describes it as "a Christian Utopian Closed Corporate Community."[5] Lockridge's Dedham may conform more closely than other towns to the ideal type we have been constructing; it is all the more useful in revealing the dynamics of social change, by which a closed corporate community becomes an open town of more or less free individuals. A striking fact about the first settlement of Dedham, Lockridge reminds us, is that despite the availability of large tracts of undivided land within the limits of the town, only about 3000 acres were divided up in the first twenty years. (The town, incidentally, originally extended all the way from the present Dedham to Wrentham and the Rhode Island border.) Yet even though this vast acreage was not immediately exploited, it represented a constant threat to the original sense of community. As population increased, and the need was felt to bring more land under cultivation, the original structures of community crumbled. Not only were people moving out to dwell beyond the range of the original compact settlement, but the new towns that were set off from the original Dedham were settled not by group action but by the initiative of individuals. In other towns, this process may have occurred even more rapidly.

The medieval organic concept of society was predicated on a relatively stable relationship between population and resources, specifically land. When the first settlers came to Massachusetts Bay, they brought with them a set of social institutions and values that had been functional back home. But the presence of a vast untamed wilderness transformed familiar institutions.

---

[5] Kenneth A. Lockridge, *A New England Town: The First Hundred Years* (New York, 1970), p. 16.

Group migration planted small settlements on the edge of the wilderness; perhaps only some sort of corporate undertaking could have done it. But afterwards, only individual initiative could conquer that wilderness.

This small historical example points to a bold generalization, namely, that individualism is a response to a fairly sudden favorable alteration in the balance between population and resources, given a particular state of technology. As a strand or motif in modern Western culture, individualism is intimately connected with the peopling of the North American continent. Ideologies do not immediately adapt to new social situations, and so it took time for the presence of land in great abundance to alter traditional institutions and patterns of thought. But by the eighteenth century, the concept of the autonomous individual was well established in American social theory, political theory, and church polity. No wonder that "the great Mr. Locke" became America's philosopher. The lands extending westward with the barest scattering of population approximated Locke's State of Nature. His argument that private property arises when the individual mixes his labor with the unappropriated bounty of nature made good sense to the American frontiersman who cleared the land with his own hands, and built a shelter without government aid or interference.

Here we may note additional justification for the use of Thomas Jefferson as one of our key symbols. For not only was he the author of the Virginia Act for Establishing Religious Freedom (1786), and the Declaration of Independence, with its Whiggish, Lockean political theory, but he wrote an early draft of what eventually became the Northwest Ordinance, and it was in his administration that the Louisiana Purchase substantially doubled the territorial extent of the United States. Jefferson did not invent individualism, nor did he create a vacant continent waiting to be exploited; but he was surely a major influence in encouraging Americans to believe that the individual is primary and society an adventitious overlay—or, in Emerson's words, that the individual is the world.

There is an ominous implication to the generalization that individualism is a response to a fairly sudden favorable alteration in the balance between population and resources. It is that the social situation that fostered individualism will be a temporary one, and so the philosophy of individualism will sooner or later become dysfunctional if not obsolete. By "sooner or later" we do not mean within the life span of an individual, but a couple of centuries perhaps—short enough in the perspective of the millennia of human history. I would venture to predict that if there are any historians around 500 years from now, they will look back on the past three centuries as a curious aberration in the history of mankind—the product of a unique combination of population, natural resources, and technology that can never come again.

Now let us try to refine the generalization already twice stated. To do so we need the help of the demographers to chart such factors as world population and per capita use of energy over the past three centuries. The exact figures may be a matter for discussion among the experts, but the general trend is surely not in dispute. Both world population and energy use have increased; since the growth rate is exponential, the increase at first seems to be very modest, but there comes a point when the curve moves rapidly upward. In the eighteenth century, world population increased 300,000,000 or 350,000,000. In the nineteenth century, the increase was perhaps 700,000,000. In the first half of the present century alone, it increased by a billion. By that time, the doubling time was less than one-third of a century.

My purpose in mentioning all this is not to remind us of the problems that the population explosion poses for us, or to argue for more money for solar energy research, or to suggest that we have got to do something about the fragile ecological systems that maintain life on this earth if we are to survive, or to warn of the social dislocations that lie not so very far down the road, or to ask whether the present inflation may be unlike other periods of inflation because it is a premonitory symptom of an oncoming ecological crisis. Those are crucial problems, but ones that others can address more effectively than I. What I am suggesting is that the value system that liberals have taken for granted, and have always assumed will be vindicated by history, is in need of overhaul along with everything else. Perhaps the population curve will not continue to rise exponentially, but a new steady-state equilibrium will be established between population and resources. Already, indeed, scarcity of particular materials has begun to restrict economic growth. Presumably we shall end up with a sigmoid curve for economic activity, in which the rising curve levels off again.

The generalization then is that individualism thrives as one moves from a steady state into a period of growth; and that it becomes dysfunctional as limits to growth come into play. When one moves from an era of abundance to the threat of scarcity, individualism can no longer be the guiding principle in social relationships, or else one ends up in the Hobbist war of each against each, "and the life of man solitary, poor, nasty, brutish, and short." If some sort of civilized existence is to survive, the individualism of the phase of growth will become vestigial, if not obsolete. That a new doctrine of individualism may emerge, relevant to the new situation, is of course a possibility. But it will not be the Lockean, Jeffersonian, Emersonian kind.

In the period of growth, precipitated by the opening up of the western world, when resources seemed superabundant compared with the demands made upon them, the individual could operate freely, with few social controls or restraints. Let us grant that the use of the forests *was* wasteful, and the exploitation of flocks of passenger pigeons *was* carried beyond the point of no return—there was more where that came from. Let us admit that that supreme individualist Henry Thoreau was careless with his campfire, and started a forest fire that he left to burn itself out— there were few other people around to be affected. Indeed, economic expansion at that time required the abandonment of earlier forms of restraint, as for example the doctrine of just price or the ban on usury.

When the population increases, however, without proportional expansion of resources, the efforts of individuals, or individual entrepreneurs, to maximize profits without regard to the common welfare will deplete the resources on which all depend, and eventually the aggrandizing individual will suffer as well. As long as there was plenty of codfish on the Grand Banks, and there were only a few fishing boats exploiting this natural reserve, individual initiative operated to increase the supply of commodities available for human support; the philosophy of individualism was functional under such circumstances. When floating fish factories swarmed over the Atlantic fisheries, and each operator sought an increased share of the catch, overfishing diminished the stock available to all. The pursuit of self-interest by each party resulted in loss, not gain.

A social environment conditioned by the fact of ecological scarcity is not going to appeal very much to those of us who have enjoyed the twilight glow of the age of affluence. The standard of living will decline for the privileged populations of the world; the revolution of rising expectations of which we used to hear will end in bitter disappointment for millions in the Third World. If the Hobbist war of all against all is avoided, social controls will be more widespread and inclusive, and probably more onerous. Individual eccentricity will be under pressure from forces making for social conformity. Political, social, and economic institutions that have developed over the past three centuries, like political democracy and industrial capitalism, will have to be reconstructed. By the same token, the usual critiques of the dominant institutions of our society, like Marxism, will be likewise obsolescent.

In *Ecology and the Politics of Scarcity*, William Ophuls states the situation thus:

> Under conditions of ecological scarcity the individual, possessing an inalienable right to pursue happiness as he defines it and exercising his liberty in a basically laissez-faire system, will inevitably produce the ruin of the commons. Accordingly, the individualistic basis of society, the concept of inalienable rights, the purely self-defined pursuit of happiness, liberty as maximum freedom of action, and laissez-faire itself all become problematic, requiring major modification or perhaps even abandonment if we wish to avert inexorable environmental degradation and eventual extinction as a civiliza-

tion. Certainly, democracy as we know it cannot conceivably survive.

So where does this leave liberal religion, as we have known it? On the verge of irrelevancy? Or still with some chance of adaptation and survival?

The predicament of liberal religion today arises in no small measure from its success in accommodating itself in earlier generations to the spirit of that age. Unitarians and Universalists sought to embody the best and most humane values of the Age of Liberalism. But the more successfully they expressed the value system of that age, the greater the risk of becoming obsolete with it.

Liberal religion articulated a value system that derived its strength from the social arrangements made possible by the discovery of the exploitable resources of the New World. But those resources were not limitless. The infinity of the private individual was plausible enough on the shores of Walden Pond, when there was no one closer than Concord Village a mile away; it is hollow rhetoric on the streets of Calcutta or in the barrios of Caracas. The progress of mankind onward and upward forever may have seemed an axiom grounded in history to James Freeman Clarke; it seems something less than that to the residents of Middletown, Pennsylvania. The principle of religious toleration was easy for Jefferson, who could not see that it did any injury for his neighbor to say there are twenty gods or no god; but the principle of toleration takes on a sharper edge when the decisive differences are not in the realm of speculative theology, but on the question of apartheid and what it is that others should be forced, despite their opinions, to do about it.

Of course the liberal tradition in religion has not been pure and unadulterated individualism. There have always been counter-currents and eddies; some religious liberals have criticized the excesses of individualism and stressed the value, significance, and requirements of religious community. We have had Henry Ware, Jr., as well as Channing; we have had Frederic Henry Hedge as well as Emerson; we have had Henry W. Bellows as well as Octavius Brooks Frothingham. But we have seldom listened to these voices for long. We have not named churches for Bellows, who believed that churches are important; we name them for Emerson, who thought them superfluous.

What is required now is a major paradigm change—to use terminology that is familiar to historians these days, and even somewhat faddish among them. The concept was introduced into our thinking by T.S. Kuhn, in his *Structure of Scientific Revolutions*. A paradigm is a conceptual structure that provides a way of organizing our perceptions, understanding our experience, and defining our problems. We see through the spectacles of the reigning paradigm; it enables us to take note of certain things in our experience, while remaining oblivious to others. But from time to time we cannot help but become aware of data the paradigm cannot handle; and eventually a change in the paradigm itself will be the result. The end of the Age of Liberalism comes when its paradigms no longer apply. Then old categories break down, and strange alliances and alignments emerge. The axioms of individualistic liberalism now no longer provide a certain guide to political decision, economic development, or socially responsible behavior.

What is now required of religious liberals if they are to play a significant role in shaping the new age? I venture only a few brief suggestions now, hopeful that once we have negotiated a paradigm shift, some of these matters will come clear. First of all, the heirs of the liberal tradition will have to re-emphasize the religious community as something requiring both commitment and discipline. This will require the shaping of a doctrine of the Church more adequate than Emerson's talking club of individualists. It means a rejection of the Jeffersonian concept of religion as a purely private concern; it means no more of the Emersonian declaration that walking along in grove and glen, however pleasant, is an adequate substitute for religious fellowship.

Second, there must be a rediscovery of worship as a corporate act, hence one in which the liturgical preferences held individually by the members of the group can never be wholly accommodated. The existence of a group imposes a discipline on its members in the rituals of worship, as in other things. Perhaps the ones who will find it hardest to accept this lesson will be those leaders of public worship who assume that a public performance put on for the benefit of the congregation, as coopted participants, is the same thing as corporate worship.

Third, there will be a rejection of the narcissism that has tainted such developments as the human potential movement, and a recognition that to be truly human is not to withdraw inward but to know how to relate to others.

Finally, in a time when social controls will establish the framework within which we can act, liberals will have to learn how to use the principles of individualism, not as though they can supply a positive sanction for the creative thrust of an expanding society, but as a critical principle when the locus of constructive power has gone elsewhere. Even in the new age there may be a social utility to individualism, but it will be a very different kind of utility when it is critical, and not constructive. There is still a place for individualism as a rallying cry against the abuses of power in institutional structures, whether political or economic. But that implies something different than the notion that by destroying oppressive institutions, greater freedom for the individual will necessarily result.

So the fate of religious liberalism rests with us. We may cling to the old paradigm, proclaim individual freedom of belief as an absolute value, and neglect of corporate worship as our inalienable right. Then we may dwindle in numbers and influence until we end up a museum piece, like the Shakers, the Schwenkfelders, and the Swedenborgians. But on the other hand, we may learn how to relate to new social forces, to master a new paradigm. If so, we may not simply assure our own survival as a segment of the Church Universal, but we may even contribute something to the humanizing of what threatens to be a far less comfortable world than the one you and I have known.